GW00420233

LONDO
CLAS

EXCELLENT BOOKS

EXCELLENT BOOKS
94 BRADFORD ROAD
WAKEFIELD
WEST YORKSHIRE WF1 2AE
TEL / FAX: (01924) 315147

First Published 1999
Reprinted 2000
Text © Richard Peace 1999
Photographs and illustrations © Richard Peace 1999

Maps © Richard Peace 1999. Based on Ordnance Survey maps, 1948 or earlier, 'One Inch' series. Town maps based on Ordnance Survey maps, 1948 or earlier, 6 inch to the mile, 'County Map' series. All maps updated and revised using the original work of the author.

ISBN 1-901464-04-0

Whilst the author has cycled and researched the route for the purposes of this guide, no responsibility can be accepted for any unforeseen circumstances encountered whilst following it. The publisher would, however, welcome information regarding any material changes and problems encountered.

Front cover photo: Grand Union Canal approaching Brentford
Rear cover photo: Family group on the Icknield Way near Princes Risborough

Printed in Great Britain by
FM Repro Ltd.
Repro House, 69 Lumb Lane
Roberttown
Liversedge
West Yorkshire WF15 7NB

CONTENTS

The Sustrans-converted railpath near Towersey (section 5)

INTRODUCTION

WHAT IS THE LONDON TO OXFORD CLASSIC?

The London to Oxford Classic links two of England's most historic and beautiful cities by bike, with the opportunity to sample the glorious countryside of the Thames Valley, the Chilterns and south-east Oxfordshire lying in between. The route is designed for leisure cyclists of all levels, be they beginners, families or experienced hands (at the very least some limited experience of leisure cycling is advised). It's ideal for a long leisurely holiday of a week to ten days. Those pushed for time can limit their sightseeing and can even do a limited section of the route, returning by train.

The route is also hopefully a contribution to the recent growth in 'green tourism', as well as being a more interesting way of seeing two of the country's top tourist spots. Countless visitors are whisked in air-conditioned buses from our capital to 'the city of dreaming spires' and for many foreign tourists it must seem this is all England consists of (with the exception, perhaps, of additional visits to Stratford-upon-Avon, Cambridge and York). If more time was taken getting from A to B, with less emphasis on the customary sprint around the 'essential' tourist hotspots visitors could see a more varied picture of the blend of ancient and modern that makes up this small but famous corner of our country. The quiet, beech-clad folds of the Chilterns and the serene beauty of the Thames have, in their own way, as much to offer as internationally recognised London and Oxford. Of course, the 'Classic' is also a new opportunity for those living hereabouts to take a fresh look at what lies around them, and to have a great time whilst doing so!

WHAT TO EXPECT

Although the route is undoubtedly challenging for beginners it has been designed to make the journey as safe and as easily navigable as possible, at the same time having plenty of places of interest and scenic interest along the way. Its main features are:

• **Over 50% off-road**. This is not a hard-core mountain-biking route as many of the trails and paths used are relatively flat and well-surfaced. The steepest off-road gradients are found on the Icknield riders' route along the Chilterns and a route using minor roads around the upland barrier is given for those who don't fancy steeper off-road riding. In any case, the Icknield riders' route is a relatively small part of the route. Much effortless off-road riding remains, especially by the side of the Thames and the Grand Union Canal.

• **Waymarking**. Although the London to Oxford Classic is not waymarked itself it uses long stretches of waymarked routes. The main routes are summarised in the table below. Appropriate directions have also been put alongside the maps in this guide to make navigation as smooth and easy as possible.

• **Avoids traffic**. Where it is necessary to venture onto the roads, quiet country lanes are used where possible. The guide alerts you to any small sections of busy or major road and gives suitable advice on minimising risk (this only happens very occasionally).

The chapter division into 8 sections of 20 to 30 miles makes for a leisurely trip with plenty of time in the day to take in exciting attractions such as Windsor Great Park, Richmond Park and the many beauty spots in the Chiltern Hills. More experienced cyclists may want to aim to cover two 'chapters' a day, which is a fair challenge. The major challenge comes on the 'return leg' in the form of the Icknield Way Riders' Route . Do not be put off by this; simply allow more time for these sections and remember what goes up must come down! Steep gradients are the exception not the rule on this route.

MAIN BIKE TRAILS USED BY THE LONDON TO OXFORD CLASSIC

Thames Cycle Route
A route designed to run alongside the Thames through much of Greater London, it overlaps with part of theThames Valley Cycle Route. Not waymarked at the time of writing, it has an interim launch date of June 2000.

Thames Valley Cycle Route
SUSTRANS. The whole length of this London-Oxford route is used, some 130 km. Although the route doesn't follow the Thames for its whole length it keeps as close as possible to the Thames Valley. Interim route and SUSTRANS map planned for 1999.

Icknield Way Riders' Route
A waymarked route for walkers, cyclists and horses. Some 23 km links the north-west side of the Chilterns with the Grand Union Canal. Some   difficult sections of the route are avoided and alternative bridleways used.

Colne Valley Trail
Nice flat cycle-paths taking you 12 km from Rickmansworth to the edge of Greater London.

SUSTRANS - THE CYCLE PATH CHARITY

Sustrans is short for sustainable transport and it is through the construction of a 6,500 mile National Cycle Network that this organisation hopes to promote this aim. Since its founding in 1980 Sustrans has seen a spectacular growth in popularity. The Thames Valley Cycle Route and the Thames Cycle Route are simply parts in the creation of such a network. Over £40 million of Millennium funds have been earmarked to help in the construction of this cycle network. Sustrans aim to promote local journeys by bike and 'green tourism'. Sustrans also relies on income from members. For further details of Sustrans services contact:

SUSTRANS HEAD OFFICE
35 King Street, Bristol BS1 4DZ
(0117) 929 0888

ROUTE GEOGRAPHY

LONDON AND OXFORD

The route in this edition starts at Putney Bridge and works its way through scenery that is gentle but arguably unequalled in its sense of serenity . The popular cycling venue of Richmond Park gives way to relaxed pedaling on the Thames towpath out to Hampton Court and the Thames Cycle Route gives way to the Thames Valley Cycle Route in the process. More central sections of the Thames Cycle Route will be included in future editions, as and when available, with the route starting in central London.

Oxford is, of course, mainly known as a university city but fittingly it is also a city where the bike plays a major role in local transport and student life! Church spires combine with the towering architecture of the colleges and other university institutions to create a lasting impression on the visitor (despite the fact they are grouped around a small but conventionally modern shopping area). At its edges there are of course the signs of 20th century growth, in the form of housing estates, light industry and business parks - especially noticeable when arriving by car. The old centre, however, is an architectural law unto itself with Gothic, Palladian, Classical and Victorian styles, to name but a few.

The Rivers Cherwell and Thames (Isis) further add to this uniqueness and there are some beautiful walks combining colleges and rivers (Magdalen and Christ Church meadows are just a couple of examples). It was only in the 20th century that industry began to compete in scale with the life of the university, which had grown over the centuries to dominate most of the city centre. In the mid-nineteenth century the major employer was still related to education in the form of the University Press but by 1913 William Morris had produced his first car here and by 1925 he was making 41% of all cars produced in the UK. Today the university's science graduates are a ready source of material for hi-tech industry, epitomised by the science park, which provides another face of this multi-faceted city.

THE THAMES

The Thames is arguably the most well-known river in Great Britain and is the longest at 210 miles. Originating from the Latin *Tamesis*, probably indicating a broad stretch of water, it has played a vital role in the nation's history and today, despite a decline in trade boats on the river, could fairly be described as the lifeblood of London. It is strange to think that the broad river at the start of the London to Oxford Classic begins life in mid-Gloucestershire, in an insignificant meadowy stream called Thames Head.

Our route follows the Thames through much of West London from Putney Bridge to the idyllic Teddington Lock, on to the rich history of Hampton Court and the rural beauty around Walton-on-Thames. Beyond here the route touches the Thames less often but there are many opportunities to sample its surrounding countryside. The historic highpoint comes alongside the Thames at Windsor and Eton before touching the river again near the more modern towns of Maidenhead and Reading . By this stage the river has become more rural and less grand; it is back at Teddington, in fact, that the river stops being tidal and becomes freshwater. After passing over the southern tip of the Chilterns, into relatively flat south-east Oxfordshire, we meet the river again at the delightful market towns of Wallingford and Abingdon.

Whatever condition the Thames is in where you meet it, be it boatyards, riverhouses, city centre grandeur or rural backwater, it is frightening to think that the river was in danger of dying completely from the mid-nineteenth century onwards. Population growth meant huge quantities of raw sewage were pumped into the 'Monster Soup'. The smell from the opaque brown fluid filling the Thames became so bad in 1858 that sheets steeped in disinfectant had to be hung in the House of Commons. The intense pollution was linked to numerous outbreaks of cholera and typhoid. The river has been gradually improved up to the present day. Sewage systems and chemical and biological treatment have very evidently greatly reduced the pollution problem.

Flooding was once a major problem but the construction of numerous embankments and the Thames Barrier at Woolwich Reach has meant the threat of a tidal surge inundating much of London is now a thing of the past. Today **leisure provision,** not trade, is the main function of the Thames alongside **water provision** for a large proportion of London's population. The punt, the favoured craft of Elizabethan water traders, is now used for relaxing and having fun. On a summer weekend, as fishermen, walkers, cyclists and boaters mingle on and around the river it's difficult to imagine the majestic Thames once in such a sorry state.

THE CHILTERNS AND SURROUNDING COUNTRYSIDE

The Chilterns derive their name from the Saxon word for chalk and it is this soft, porous rock that gives these hills their beautifully rounded character. The chalk base is topped in places with clay and flints (look out for large nodules of the latter as hitting one unaware can easily tip you off your bike). The steeply sided coombes were formed after the main bulk of the hills, during the Ice Age.

About a quarter of the Chilterns retains dense tree coverage, although not of the original oak which was cleared in Neolithic times. Today beech trees dominate, some growing more than 100 feet tall, constructing a leafy canopy in the process and blocking out much light from the woodland floor. This lack of sunlight leaves the forest floor strangely denuded of other greenery in many places but unusual flora and fauna do survive. The Chilterns are known for orchids, some of which don't appear anywhere else in Britain and if you are lucky you might catch a glimpse of a muntjac deer. The beeches were introduced deliberately, several centuries ago, both to provide charcoal fuel for London's growing population and as a source of wood for a developing furniture industry.

Despite such change the Chilterns retain many traditional villages, based around the water supply in the coombes and the land has been spared the worst excesses of the intensive agriculture that now so dominates the Vale of Aylesbury below. Harder to work than the vale, the chalky slopes have retained some ancient landscape features such as hedgerows many hundreds of years old.

Most ancient of all is the Icknield Way, an ancient neolithic track that was used to link East Anglia with Dorset several thousand years ago. On meeting the Chilterns it split into the upper and lower Icknield Ways. The upper Icknield Way (probably the winter route) is now substantially the same as the Ridgeway and some sections of this are followed as the Icknield Way riders' route, covered in chapter 6. The lower Icknield Way (probably the summer route), although retaining its name in places, was largely adopted by the Romans and later metalled for cars.

GETTING THERE AND AWAY

Arrive by train! This is the message Sustrans are trying to get across and rightly so. There are problems in taking bikes on trains (space is often limited on main lines where bikes are put in separate coaches and on branch lines usually you must simply wait and see if there is space in one of the normal carriages) but with a little planning few problems should arise. Privatisation has also lead to divergence in rules about carrying bikes on trains; some carriers may make a great effort to accommodate you whilst others might have unhelpful restrictions. The best rules are to **book ahead as early as possible** on main line journeys and on branch lines get to the guard as quickly as possible! In practice problems are likely to arise either in the morning or evening rush hour when little space is available, and even here the density of passengers varies dramatically depending on the particular journey. A summary of the present situation follows but you should always check up-to-date arrangements.

• On Inter-City journeys from the rest of the UK to London bike reservations are necessary and generally cost £3. Again check details of your particular journey.
• For a summary of stations on the route and an overview of the network see the map overleaf. The bike policies of the train companies operating in the area of the London - Oxford Classic are as follows:

Thames Trains (Paddington to Maidenhead, Reading and Oxford). Bikes go free. Some services have special areas put aside for bikes (marked with bike symbols on carriages). Bikes not allowed on trains due to arrive at or depart from Paddington, Monday to Friday, 7.45 to 9.45 a.m. and 4.30 to 6.30 p.m. Enquiries (0118) 9579453).
South West Trains (Waterloo to Basingstoke, Guildford and Oxford). Bikes go free on local services with a £3 charge on inter-city services. No bikes on trains to and from Waterloo, Monday to Friday, during same restricted hours as Thames Trains. Enquiries (0345) 484950. Note this is also the national rail enquiry line.
Chiltern Trains (Marylebone, London to Aylesbury and Banbury). Bikes go free. Bikes not allowed on busy commuter trains. Enquiries (01296) 332100.
Silverline Trains (Euston to Watford, King's Langley, Hemel Hempstead, Berkhamsted and Tring) Bikes free on local journeys but Monday to Friday rush hour ban before 9.30 a.m. into Euston and 4 to 7 p.m. out of Euston. (01923) 207258
London Underground Bikes are allowed, free of charge, only on the shallow lines i.e. Circle, District and Hammersmith and City. They are not permitted Monday to Friday, 7.30 to 9.30 a.m. and 4.00 p.m. to 7.00 p.m. On other 'deep' lines bikes are only allowed on certain small sections. London Travel Information (0171) 9183015.

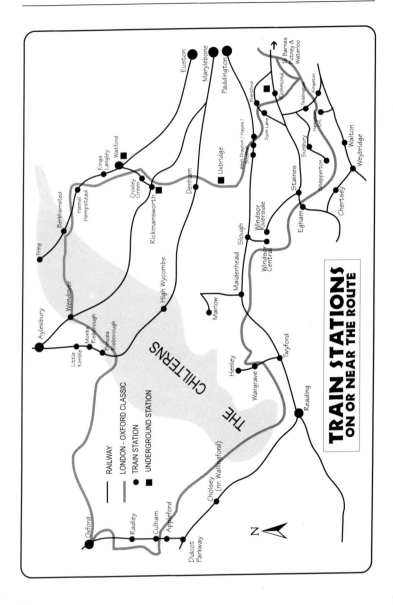

TRAIN STATIONS
ON OR NEAR THE ROUTE

RAILWAY

LONDON - OXFORD CLASSIC

● TRAIN STATION

■ UNDERGROUND STATION

THE CHILTERNS

N

Euston · Marylebone · Paddington · Richmond · Barnes · Putney & · Waterloo · Brentford · Kingston · Teddington · Kings Langley · Watford · Croxley Green · Syon Lane · West Drayton / Hayes / Southall · Uxbridge · Sunbury · Walton · Weybridge · Shepperton · Staines · Chertsey · Berkhamsted · Hemel Hempstead · Rickmansworth · Denham · Windsor Riverside · Egham · Tring · Wendover · High Wycombe · Maidenhead · Slough · Windsor Central · Aylesbury · Little Kimble · Monks Risborough · Princes Risborough · Marlow · Twyford · Henley · Wargrave · Reading · Oxford · Radley · Culham · Appleford · Cholsey (nr. Wallingford) · Didcot Parkway

10

Arriving in Putney by train is easy. Out of London centre it is reached from Waterloo. **Putney Bridge Underground Station** is just to the north of the bridge on the District Line.

PREPARATION

The Thames Cycle Route and the Thames Valley Cycle Route are intended for leisure riders, commuters and those making other local journeys. Both routes enjoy beautiful scenery whilst linking major centres of population. Although the return leg avoids major towns until it hits the Grand Union Canal it is also suitable for leisure and commuting. This guide is split into 8 'day' sections, ranging from 18 to 27 miles, aimed at novice cyclists or those with plenty of time who want to take in some of the attractions. 10 days is a comfortable period of time for a leisurely holiday along the whole route and allows for a couple of rest days. Those with less time can aim to do a suitable length of the route and return by train, making use of the area's excellent rail network. Some keen cyclists, especially those with previous experience of the route, can complete it much more quickly. Section start and finish points are as near as possible to centres of population where accommodation is plentiful, but this is not always possible when trying to keep section distances reasonably even. It is still advisable to book accommodation as far in advance as practicable; this is especially the case if you are completing the route in summer or you are planning to stay in smaller settlements with only limited accommodation. Those wanting to camp along the way should certainly have some previous cycling experience and allow extra time as the extra equipment weight slows down even the fittest cyclist quite noticeably.

One of the most important factors in preparation is to have a realistic idea of what daily mileage you are comfortable in achieving; the London - Oxford Classic has a lot of flat easy cycling with more challenging sections climbing over the Chilterns (especially so if you use the 'mountain bike' option on section 6). Also bear in mind several sections are due to be upgraded over the coming months and years and some short but potentially muddy sections remain. Adjust time estimates accordingly. The route profile and description at the beginning of each section give a good idea of what to expect.

CHECKLIST Basic essentials - there is a huge range of specialist cycling gear available. The list assumes you are staying B&B.

Clothing (winter / summer options included)
Helmet
High wicking inner layer (doesn't soak up sweat)
Cycle shirt and / or fleece top
Waterproof outer (preferably breathable-well known makes are Goretex and Ceplex)
Gloves
Padded shorts
Thermal leggings
Tracksuit bottoms
Waterproof trousers
Boots / trainers / cycling shoes
At the least one change of clothing based on the above
Sun hat / glasses / block

Tool Kit ('Multi-tools' may include several of these)
Small screwdriver
Small adjustable spanner
Allen keys (4,5,6 mm at least)
Pump
Spare brake blocks
Strong tape for quick repair
Small container chain and gear lubricant
Chain link extractor
Puncture kit & new inner tube

Other Essentials
Guide and maps (see map section)
Water bottle
Telephone contact of friends/family for emergency
Toilet paper
Survival bag (used to keep warm if stuck in foul weather conditions)

Bike lights
Money
Washing kit
Towel
Small first aid kit
Prescribed medication

This list will have obvious additions depending on the person; you may be camping or you may be enough of a mechanic to be able to replace a variety of parts.

MAINTENANCE

If you set off with a well-maintained bike the chances are that you won't need any of the tools or spares you take. A bike in good condition is especially important for such a long distance route. The most basic check should include the following list and if in any doubt about the state of your bike get it checked over properly at a good bike shop.

Important safety checks - do not neglect them!

Brake check - you should only be able to squeeze in front and rear brake levers a centimetre or two and braking response should be nice and sharp. Check brake blocks aren't rubbing on wheel rims, or even worse, tyres.
Brake cables - check that front and rear brake cables are not fraying. If they are replace them immediately.
Brake blocks - check that when you brake the blocks hit only the wheel rim, not the tyre and that there is plenty of wear left in the block.
Tyres - should be inflated to manufacturer's recommended pressure (as a rough guide you should just be able to depress the tyre when squeezing it). Check there is adequate tread.

Make sure the following are **lubricated**: front and rear brake pivots, moving parts of front and rear gear mechanisms, chain, brake lever pivots, entry and exit points of all cables. Keep these points well-lubricated during the ride.

Appropriate **screws and bolts** should be tight and you should check all gears are shifting properly.

For a full guide to buying and maintaining a bike see Haynes 'The Bike Book'.

CARRYING LOADS

Panniers are the ideal way to carry your extra gear. Small amounts of gear can be put in bum bags and the smaller seat and frame bags that fit around the bike or in handlebar bags or even a very small backpack. However, unless travelling very light in summer, you will probably need panniers. Start off with rear panniers which sit on a frame over the rear wheel. Large amounts of extra gear will go in 'low rider' front panniers either side of the front forks. At all costs don't overload handlebar bags or a backpack - this will dangerously affect handling and balance.

Go by bike and train; truly sustainable transport!

SIGNING & STAMPING

An interim version of the Thames Valley Cycle Route should be up and running by the middle of 1999. Do not confuse it with the Thames Path National Trail which is a walking route! Between London and Reading look out for the National Route number 4 signs (a white number 4 on a red background). Between Reading and Oxford you change on to National Route 5. Signs change accordingly but the waymarking style remains the same (see the sign on the front cover). However, from Oxford to London you will be more reliant on the text directions unless you happen to be following part of a route already signed such as the Colne Valley Way (see page 5 for full details of other routes). IMPORTANT NOTE: The Thames Valley Cycle Route was still partly under design and construction at the time this guide was written (with the assistance of Sustrans). You are therefore strongly advised to use a copy of the Sustrans map alongside this guide as a further aid on the London to Oxford section. Signing is due to be completed on the route by mid-1999. The route maps indicate where new sections are due to come on line in the future and alternative routes have been given that can be cycled now. On some small parts of the route you may find a conflict between route directions and signing as last minute changes could have occurred. Should this be the case you may either continue to follow the route directions or the signs as both options will join up again.

USING THIS GUIDE AND OTHER MAPS

Although you should be able to complete the London - Oxford Classic with an up-to-date edition of this book you are strongly advised to take other maps. You should, at least, take the Sustrans map to the Thames Valley Cycle Route, due out in June 2000. If not available you will have to rely on the OS Landranger maps (1:50,000 scale) listed below. The return leg from Oxford to London is not an official Sustrans route and is therefore not waymarked (although much of it uses shorter existing trails such as the Colne Valley Trail which are waymarked).

No. 176 - West London area (section 1, part of section 2, part of section 7 and section 8)
No. 175 - Reading & Windsor (part of section 2 and section 3)
No. 164 - Oxford & surrounding area (section 4 and part of section 5)
No. 165 - Aylesbury & Leighton Buzzard (part of section 5 and section 6)
No. 166 - Luton & Hertford (part of section 7)

MAP KEY

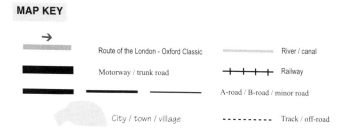

→ Route of the London - Oxford Classic

Motorway / trunk road

A-road / B-road / minor road

City / town / village

River / canal

+ + + + Railway

- - - - - - - - - Track / off-road

B&B / CAMPSITE KEY

Information is based on individual questionnaires from owners; please confirm the information whilst booking. Other accommodation providers are listed with briefer details where they have not returned questionnaires. Brief details are also given of camping sites indicated by a ⋏ sign in the text.

B&B Abbreviations - prices are per person per night based on a double room.

£ = Under £10   ££ = Under £15   £££ = Under £20   ££££ = Under £25
£££££ = Over £25   PL = Packed Lunches (other meals also detailed) DR = Drying Facilities LAU = Laundry Facilities SEC = Secure Bike Place WKSH = Workshop facilities.

The quiet side of Oxford discovered on the London-Oxford Classic

1 PUTNEY - STAINES

Section Distance 23miles / 37km   **Off-road** 19 miles / 30.5km

The Route A mix of off-road path and quiet minor roads through some of West London's more exclusive suburbs starts the London to Oxford Classic. Richmond Park involves a small climb to White Lodge but out of the park you are soon back alongside the Thames from where it's largely flat off-road cycling to Staines. Although it sounds like a cliche, many Thames-side spots do seem to hark back to a previous era when the pace of life was slower. The contrast in scenery is incredible, from the glorious views in Richmond Park to the grandeur of Hampton Court Palace and the tree-lined tranquility of our best known river.

PUTNEY TO RICHMOND

• **Putney riverside** reflects the fact that Putney Bridge is the start of the Boat Race between Oxford and Cambridge Universities (it finishes at Mortlake). Rowed annually in March, the Boat Race attracts large crowds. Racing on the Thames grew out of the trade of oarsmen on the river (in Queen Anne's time there were around 10,000 licensed 'watermen' on the tidal reaches of the river). Numerous boat sheds show rowing's popularity on this stretch of the river.
Banks Lloyds and Natwest on High St., both with cashpoints.
⌚ W.F. Holdsworth, 132 Lower Richmond Road, Putney (0181) 7881060.
• **The Wetland Centre** on Queen Elizabeth Walk is scheduled to open in spring 2000. A unique creation for water-loving birds from the Wildfowl and Wetlands Trust (creators of Slimbridge). Created from scratch on the site of an old reservoir, it promises 'high-tech' birdwatching facilities! For details ring (0181) 8768995.

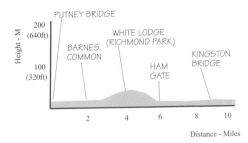

• **Fulham Palace**, standing on the northern side of the Thames, next to Putney Bridge, and enclosed by a bank of trees, is home of the Bishop of London. Visible from the path after leaving Embankment is **Fulham football ground**.

• **Richmond Park** Superb blend of deer park, woodland and water amounting to Europe's largest city park. Originally a **royal hunting ground**, it is now criss-crossed by tracks and paths, the wide open spaces making you forget you are anywhere near London. Other royal parks were made into formal gardens but many parts of Richmond are still essentially a wild habitat. The 2,400 acres was first enclosed by Charles I. **White Lodge**, passed on the route, was the birthplace of Edward VIII and is now home to the Royal Ballet School. Originally built as a hunting lodge for George II who would hunt wild turkey, specially introduced into the park as they were easy to hit! The park deer are still culled to produce venison. The **Pen Ponds** are home to numerous fish and birds. (Details of other attractions are given on the return route which follows different paths through Richmond Park. See page 98). ⚲ Original Bicycle Hire Co. near Roehampton Gate, Richmond Park (0777) 5884848.

PUTNEY TO RICHMOND - ACCOMMODATION

3 Ferry Road, Barnes (0181) 7481561
21 Vicarage Road, East Sheen (0181) 8766516
Anna Guest House, 36-38 Church Road, Richmond (0181) 9405237
Shandon House, 37 Church Road, Richmond (0181) 9405000
4 Church Road, Richmond (0181) 9485852
446 Upper Richmond Road West, Richmond (0181) 8783268
Idono, 41 Church Road, Richmond (0181) 9485852

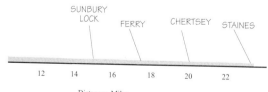

Distance - Miles

RICHMOND TO STAINES

• After Ham you join the river near the pretty **Teddington Lock**, an area boasting the longest weir and the largest lock system on the Thames. Above this point the river ceases to be tidal. South of here the Port of London Authority is responsible for the river. ⅋ Kingston Cycles, 48 Kingston Rd., Kingston (0181) 5492559. Thameside Cycles, Mkt Pl., Kingston (0181) 5472761.

• **Hampton Court Palace** Started by Cardinal Wolesley, and added to by Henry VIII and William III (who engaged Christopher Wren), this is one of England's most distinctive and beautiful royal palaces. Highlights include King's Apartments, Riverside Gardens with the famous maze, Henry VIII's superb State Apartments and an amazing collection of art. Admission charge. Opening details (0181) 7819500.

• Between Hampton Court Bridge and Chertsey the ride is dominated by **classic English riverscapes** that could hardly be anywhere else but the Thames. The view of Hampton from the Surrey bank boasts a church steeple and Garrick's villa. Further on at **Sunbury** there are some fine boathouses and residences, again on the opposite bank.

• Like Sunbury, **Walton-on-Thames** started life as grand out-of-town estates of important Londoners but has since had its character much destroyed by residential development. The **Anglers** and **Swan** pubs are handily next to the river. **Walton Bridge** was intended only as a temporary bridge but is still in use today. Shortly before Shepperton ferry look out for the unusual D'Oyly Carte Island, with operatic connections. ⅋ Walton Cycles, 9-11 The Centre, Walton-on-Thames (01932) 221424.

• **Shepperton** is centred around an attractive square with church (for a look turn right up the road after the ferry crossing instead of left onto the route). **King's Head** pub in the village square.

• **Chertsey** Very attractive town centre, largely eighteenth century, with the few remains of a medieval abbey behind the church. Small but interesting town museum includes medieval Chertsey tiles and displays of costume, porcelain and painting. Free admission. (01932) 565764. The elegant **Chertsey Bridge** dates from the late eighteenth century.

• Once predominantly a market town, **Staines** unfortunately sprawled outwards and now suffers from the homogenising effects of modern housing and light industry. The Old Town Hall now houses a diverse arts programme. Church Street retains the feel of old Staines more than any other. The granite **Staines Bridge** was designed by the Rennie Brothers, sons of famous engineer John. **Banks** All major branches on High St. ⅋ Action Bikes, Unit 1 Fairfield Av., Staines (01784) 440666.

RICHMOND TO STAINES - ACCOMMODATION

23 Seymour Rd, East Molesey (0181) 9410436
Meadowcroft, 3 Spencer Rd, East Molesey (0181) 7831426
30 Lawrence Road, Hampton (0181) 2550595. ££££-DR-SEC-Basic tools.
21 Ambleside Avenue, Walton-on-Thames (01932) 222904. £££-PL-DR-LAU-SEC-Tools
Cassita, 33 Clarence Rd, Walton-on-Thames (01932) 240748
Town Hall Tavern, Chertsey (01932) 563045
Albany House, 2 Glebe Road, Staines (01784) 441223
39 Penton Road, Staines (01784) 458787. ££££-DR-SEC.
Clivesden, 37 Gloucester Drive, Staines (01784) 464858
Rose Villa Guest House, 146 Commercial Rd, Staines (01784) 458855

Δ **Paxmead Riverside Base**, Dockett Eddy Lane, Shepperton (01932) 244212. Advance booking essential. April - Oct. **Chertsey Camping and Caravan Club Site**, Bridge Road, Chertsey (01932) 562405. Discounts to members of Camping and Caravan Club. Minimum 3 nights if booking in advance (which is essential in July / August!). **Laleham Park Camping Site**, Thameside, Laleham (01932) 564149. April - Sept.

The grand facade of Hampton Court Palace (section 1)

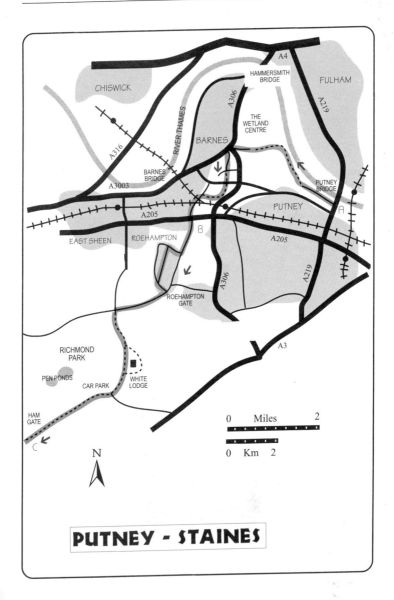

PUTNEY - STAINES

DIRECTION TIPS

A - B From the south side of Putney Bridge head on Embankment, keeping the Thames on your R. The road soon becomes a riverside path. At the first opportunity after passing Fulham football ground on the opposite bank go L, through a set of metal gates to pass sports fields then the Wetland Centre. At the end of Queen Elizabeth Walk head across the road junction onto Elm Grove Road. At the end of this road jink R then L onto a path over Barnes Common. Across Mill Lane keep on the Common track to emerge by Station Road. Down Station Road go R in front of Barnes Station then pick up the path between the railway line and the cricket ground. At the end of the path go L onto the cycle path on the R-hand side of Vine Road and over two level crossings to come to a major road junction. Head straight across onto the cycle lane on Priory Lane.

B - C After passing the sports ground on the R go R down Bank Lane and first L onto Roehampton Gate. At the end of Roehampton Gate enter Richmond Park via the side gate and onto the cycle track next to the road Go across the mini-roundabout. At the next junction go L (signed 'White Lodge only'). Pass through the woods to White Lodge, ignoring any turnings on the L. A good view opens up across Pen Ponds before meeting a car park. Through the car park go R (signed 'Isabella / Ham Gate'). At the next crossroads go straight across, onto the cycle track, and exit the park through Ham Gate.

War memorial at Coopers Hill (section 1)

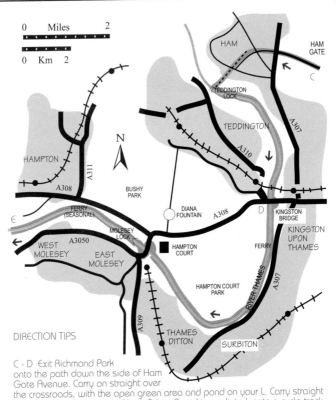

DIRECTION TIPS

C - D Exit Richmond Park
onto the path down the side of Ham
Gate Avenue. Carry on straight over
the crossroads, with the open green area and pond on your L. Carry straight
onto Lock Rd. At the end of Lock Rd go R and immediate L onto a cycle track.
Follow the track in a straight line, over the next two roads, and onto a
woodland track, following your nose to meet the River Thames near the
footbridge above Teddington Lock. Go L onto the upper of the two riverside
paths. Follow the river on your R until, just after passing under a rail bridge,
you come to a road in Kingston.
D - E L by Outrigger pub and R to work your way round car park to road
bridge. Immediately over the bridge go L onto Barge Walk to come alongside
the river on your L. Simply follow the riverside to Hampton Court Bridge, just
post the palace. Cross the bridge and immediate R onto Riverbank and bear
R to join the riverside path by Molesey Lock. Continue to follow the riverside
path through Hurst Park.

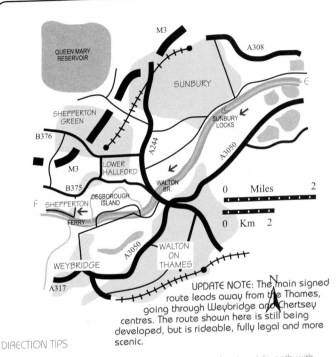

UPDATE NOTE: The main signed route leads away from the Thames, going through Weybridge and Chertsey centres. The route shown here is still being developed, but is rideable, fully legal and more scenic.

DIRECTION TIPS

€ - F From the Hurst Park area simply continue on the riverside path with the river on your R, passing the splendid boathouses of Sunbury on the opposite bank. Pass the Anglers pub at Walton and continue by the river to come under Walton Bridge. Just past Eyot House on a small island take the ferry across the river by ringing the bell.

FERRY OPENING HOURS Summer: Mon-Fri 8.30 - 6.30 Sat 9 - 6.30
                                           Sun 10 - 5.30
                        Winter: Mon - Fri 8.30 - 5.30 Sat 9 - 5.30
                                           Sun 10 - 5.30
Across the river head L on the road (YOU MUST CURRENTLY PUSH YOUR BIKE UP THIS ONE WAY STREET - a contra-flow bike lane will be installed).

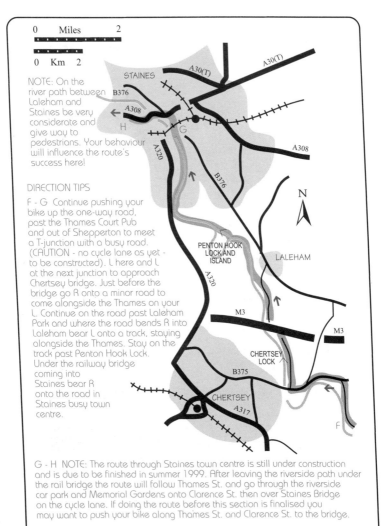

0   Miles   2

0   Km   2

NOTE: On the river path between Laleham and Staines be very considerate and give way to pedestrians. Your behaviour will influence the route's success here!

DIRECTION TIPS

F - G Continue pushing your bike up the one-way road, past the Thames Court Pub and out of Shepperton to meet a T-junction with a busy road. (CAUTION - no cycle lane as yet - to be constructed). L here and L at the next junction to approach Chertsey bridge. Just before the bridge go R onto a minor road to come alongside the Thames on your L. Continue on the road past Laleham Park and where the road bends R into Laleham bear L onto a track, staying alongside the Thames. Stay on the track past Penton Hook Lock. Under the railway bridge coming into Staines bear R onto the road in Staines busy town centre.

STAINES

A30(T)

A30(T)

B376

A308

H

G

A320

B376

A308

N

PENTON HOOK LOCK AND ISLAND

LALEHAM

A320

M3

M3

CHERTSEY LOCK

B375

CHERTSEY

A317

F

G - H NOTE: The route through Staines town centre is still under construction and is due to be finished in summer 1999. After leaving the riverside path under the rail bridge the route will follow Thames St. and go through the riverside car park and Memorial Gardens onto Clarence St. then over Staines Bridge on the cycle lane. If doing the route before this section is finalised you may want to push your bike along Thames St. and Clarence St. to the bridge.

24

Old timber and brick house in Dorney (section 2)

2 STAINES - WARGRAVE

Section Distance 26 miles / 41.5 km   **Off-road** 15.5 miles / 25 km

The Route A section of superb contrasts; after climbing to the moving Air Forces Memorial on Coopers Hill you can visit stately Windsor Great Park, then Windsor itself, dominated by the grand royal castle. The quaint old villages of Dorney and Bray precede your passage through the mainly modern Maidenhead. The fine viewpoint at the top of Bowsey Hill heralds a welcome descent into the attractive town of Wargrave. Be aware this is one of the longest sections and also includes some climbing. At the time of writing the section between Altmore and Knowl Hill was prone to much mud after heavy rain or in winter. This will change when Sustrans begin their programme of resurfacing.

STAINES TO WINDSOR

• The **Air Forces Memorial** on top of Coopers Hill commemorates 20,000 airmen with no known grave and a climb up the tower gives superb views of Windsor Castle and seven counties. A visit will stay with you for a long time. Free admission but please respect the code of conduct posted at the entrance.
• **Magna Carta and John F. Kennedy Memorials** are down a footpath behind Brunel University Campus (just off the route - no biking).
• **Windsor Great Park** is made up of an enormous 4800 acres of grassland, woodland and ponds. Much of the landscaping was done in the 18th century by 'Butcher' Cumberland, the Duke responsible for the massacre of Scots troops at Culloden. His one time residence, **Cumberland Lodge,** is passed en route. **The Village** was completed in 1951and doubles as the estate administration. If you have time to explore the park away from the route more attractions are on the map opposite. **Fox & Hounds Inn** by Bishop's Gate entrance does food (01784) 433098.

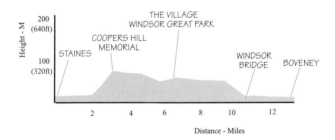

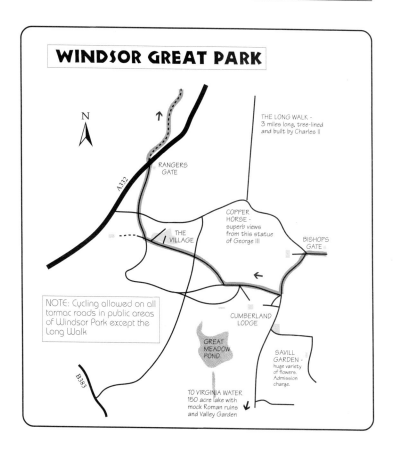

WINDSOR GREAT PARK

N

RANGERS GATE

A332

THE VILLAGE

COPPER HORSE - superb views from this statue of George III

THE LONG WALK - 3 miles long, tree-lined and built by Charles II

BISHOPS GATE

NOTE: Cycling allowed on all tarmac roads in public areas of Windsor Park except the Long Walk

CUMBERLAND LODGE

B383

GREAT MEADOW POND

SAVILL GARDEN - huge variety of flowers. Admission charge.

TO VIRGINIA WATER 150 acre lake with mock Roman ruins and Valley Garden

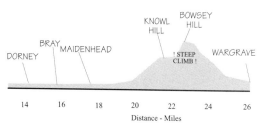

DORNEY

BRAY MAIDENHEAD

KNOWL HILL

BOWSEY HILL

! STEEP CLIMB !

WARGRAVE

14   16   18   20   22   24   26

Distance - Miles

WINDSOR AND ETON - HISTORY AND ATTRACTIONS

• **Windsor Castle** lies at the heart of the town of Windsor. It is the largest castle in England and is really a fortress, a royal home and a religious institution all blended together. Seriously damaged by fire in 1992, the castle was reopened in 1997. It was only ever seriously besieged once, during the reign of King John; in any case, formidable defences, such as the **Curfew Tower** with its 13 feet thick basement wall, would have made any medieval siege a Herculean task. Besides the Curfew Tower Henry III also added the enormous **Round Tower**. **St. George's Chapel**, started in the fifteenth century, is one of the most splendid churches in England. There are numerous chapels, monuments and windows but the richly-embossed roof is what really strikes the first-time visitor. The **State Apartments** are usually occupied by the Queen, when in residence, and are full of lavish furniture and works of art. St. George's Hall is still used for banquets by the Knights of the Garter. **Queen Mary's Dolls' House** is a work of art in itself, standing over 8 feet tall with every detail crafted to scale. These are just a few main points of interest as the castle deserves a book to itself. Admission charge. For opening details call (01753) 868286 or (01753) 831118.
• Although the town of **Windsor** lives very much in the shadow of the castle it has plenty of its own attractions. The compact streets on the south side of the castle hold most of the attractive old buildings whilst on the north-west side the town slopes pleasantly down to the Thames and the picturesque **Windsor Bridge. Queen Charlotte Street** claims to be the shortest in England. Amongst timber-framed buildings in the old quarter are the **Guildhall, Nell Gwynne's House** and **St. John's Church**. There are daily marches of the **Castle Guard** from Victoria Barracks to the castle. Look out for the **Household Cavalry Museum** showing the regiment's military history. The old station buildings of **Windsor and Eton Central Station** have been tastefully renovated for shops and restaurants. Between Barry Avenue and Windsor Bridge you can take **river trips**.
• **Eton** is just to the north of the route, over Windsor Bridge. **Eton College** is at the top of the High St. and from the **Museum of Eton Life** you can see pupils and masters in distinctive dress during term time as well as displays on past college life, including a birch. (01753) 869991. **The Brewhouse Gallery** houses a changing selection from the College's Art Gallery and Egyptian antiquities. England's most famous school was founded in 1440 by Henry VI and was lavishly endowed by royalty from the start. The **High Street** is a feast for those interested in antiques and specialist shops.

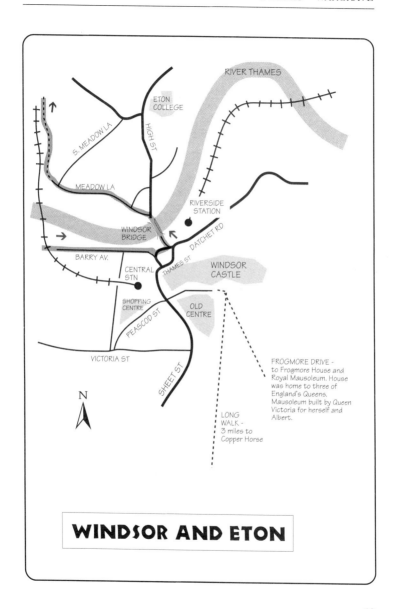

RIVER THAMES

ETON COLLEGE

S. MEADOW LA.

HIGH ST

MEADOW LA

RIVERSIDE STATION

WINDSOR BRIDGE

DATCHET RD

BARRY AV.

CENTRAL STN

THAMES ST

WINDSOR CASTLE

SHOPPING CENTRE

OLD CENTRE

PEASCOD ST

VICTORIA ST

SHEET ST

N

FROGMORE DRIVE -
to Frogmore House and
Royal Mausoleum. House
was home to three of
England's Queens.
Mausoleum built by Queen
Victoria for herself and
Albert.

LONG
WALK -
3 miles to
Copper Horse

WINDSOR AND ETON

WINDSOR - ACCOMMODATION

62 Queens Road (01753) 866036. £££ and up-DR-LAU-SEC.
48 Clarence Rd (01753) 855062
93 Dedworth Rd (01753) 862033
3 Withey Close (01753) 860485
The Arches, 9 York Road (01753) 869268
Youth Hostel, Edgeworth House, Mill Lane (01753) 861710. ££. DR-LAU-SEC.

WINDSOR - OTHER INFORMATION

Tourist Information 24 High St. (01753) 743900
Hospital No A&E facilities in Windsor. The nearest are 4 miles away at Wexham Park Hospital, Wexham St., Wexham, Slough (01753) 633000
Banks All major banks with cashpoints on Peascod / High / Thames Streets.
🚲 Stows, 209 Dedworth Rd. (01753) 862734. Windsor Cycle Hire, Alexandra Grdns., Alma Rd. (01753) 830220.

WINDSOR TO WARGRAVE

• Out of Windsor the route comes alongside the arches of the snake-like **Slough-Windsor Viaduct**, the longest series of brick arches in the world.
• Heading towards Boveney Lock near Eton Wick there are superb views back towards the Windsor skyline. **Dorney's** main street is lined with brick and timber houses and the minor road followed by the route also houses the Church of St. James and **Dorney Court**, a beautifully irregular manor house dating from the 15th century. The first pineapple in England was grown here!
• **Bray** is a cluster of attractive housing and inns full of character. The church boasts splendid brasses and the smaller building to the north of it, in the churchyard, has been variously a chantry chapel, school, workhouse, prison and a drying room for eel nets. **Jesus Hospital** is a group of 28 almshouses (visitors may see the chapel). The **Fish Inn** and **Hind's Head** serve food.
• **Maidenhead** is a residential and commuter town with only traces of its former character, providing a useful shopping centre. It was once a coaching stop-off between London and Bath and the **1777 bridge** to the east of the centre, still used by motor traffic, once saw 500 horses passing over it daily. Further south on the Thames is the precarious-looking **Brunel railway bridge**, crossing the river in just two spans and known as the sounding arch because of its echo. It can be seen from the road bridge. **Banks** Natwest, Barclays, Lloyds and Midland banks (cashpoints) on High Street. Link machine on Market St. 🚲 The Bike Shack, 87a Furze Platt Rd. (01628) 633075.

• Out of Maidenhead you see Berkshire at its most rural. Tracks across open fields lead to the village of **Knowl Hill**, deriving its name from the hill view point at the centre of the village, just south of the A4. The **Seven Stars pub** and a cafe are by the route. The **Royal Oak** and **Ring O'Bells** pubs are on the A4, to the east of the route.

• **Wargrave** is a pretty village, situated on a beautiful reach of the Thames. The modern **church** incorporates the remains of the one burnt down in 1914 by suffragettes because the vicar refused to omit the word obey from the marriage ceremony. The churchyard holds the **Hannen Mausoleum** by Lutyens. The attractive **Woodclyffe Hall** in the High Street houses most of the village's public events. Several handy shops and pubs are on the High St.

WINDSOR TO WARGRAVE - ACCOMMODATION

Bradgate, 269 Courthouse Road, Maidenhead (01628) 624280. £££/£-PL-DR-LAU-SEC.
Foxleigh Guest House, 48 Birdwood Rd, Maidenhead (01628) 670198
Gables End, 4 Gables Close, Maidenhead (01628) 639630
Braywick Grange, 100 Braywick Rd, Maidenhead (01628) 625915
Hillcrest Guest House, 19 Craufurd Rise, Maidenhead (01628) 620086
The Bird In Hand, Bath Road, Knowl Hill (01628) 826622
Linden Place, Kiln Green (0118) 9404808
Copper Beeches Guest House, Kiln Green (0118) 9402929
Somewhere to Stay, Loddon Acres, Bath Road (0118) 9345880
Appletree Cottage, Backsideans, Wargrave (0118) 9404306
Windy Brow, 204 Victoria Rd, Wargrave (0118) 9403336
Inverlodden Cottage, Ferry Lane, Wargrave (0118) 9402230
Martens House, Willow Lane, Wargrave (0118) 9403707

Δ **Amerden Caravan and Camping Site**, Old Marsh Lane, Dorney Reach (01628) 627461. April - Oct.

The route follows the Windsor - Slough rail viaduct (section 2)

The view from Bowsey Hill (section 2)

The picturesque church at Bray (section 2)

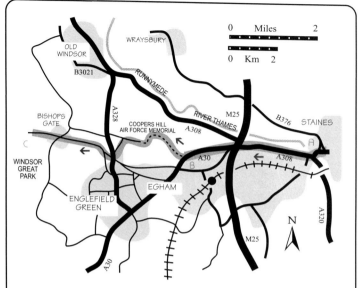

DIRECTION TIPS

A -B Over Egham Bridge come to a roundabout and go R, onto the cycle lane on the A308 towards Egham. Stay on the roadside cycle lane until you have passed under the M25. Just under this major motorway bridge pick up the cycle lane alongside the A30 (signed Basingstoke and Camberley). You may want to make a detour into Egham, signed on the exit before the A30. As the next roundabout comes into view ahead of you look for a track on the opposite side of the road (use the crossing point nearer the roundabout, it is dangerous to cross here).

B - C Climb up this earth track (possibly muddy), passing National Trust 'Runnymede' signs. Continue onto the road by the Air Forces Memorial after a stiff climb. The road splits by Brunel University's Runnymede Campus where you go L to meet the main road. Head straight over the main road onto Bishopsgate Road and continue on this road to come to the white gates that mark the entrance to Windsor Great Park. Go through the pedestrian gate and onto the excellent and quiet tarmac road in the park.

STAINES - WARGRAVE

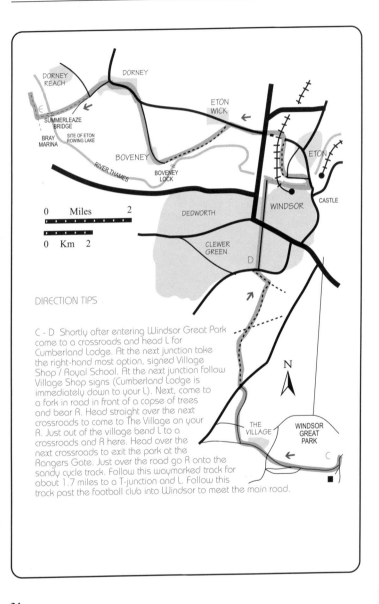

DORNEY
REACH

DORNEY

ETON
WICK

SUMMERLEAZE
BRIDGE

BRAY
MARINA

SITE OF ETON
ROWING LAKE

BOVENEY

RIVER THAMES

BOVENEY
LOCK

ETON

CASTLE

WINDSOR

0   Miles   2

0   Km   2

DEDWORTH

CLEWER
GREEN

D

DIRECTION TIPS

C - D Shortly after entering Windsor Great Park
come to a crossroads and head L for
Cumberland Lodge. At the next junction take
the right-hand most option, signed Village
Shop / Royal School. At the next junction follow
Village Shop signs (Cumberland Lodge is
immediately down to your L). Next, come to
a fork in road in front of a copse of trees
and bear R. Head straight over the next
crossroads to come to The Village on your
R. Just out of the village bend L to a
crossroads and R here. Head over the
next crossroads to exit the park at the
Rangers Gate. Just over the road go R onto the
sandy cycle track. Follow this waymarked track for
about 1.7 miles to a T-junction and L. Follow this
track past the football club into Windsor to meet the main road.

N

THE
VILLAGE

WINDSOR
GREAT
PARK

C

D - E Jink R then L onto Bulkeley Av. At the end of the avenue go R then immediate L onto York Avenue then bear R onto the cycleway, under the dual carriageway. Simply continue on Vansittart Rd. over several crossroads to its end. Head R at the T-junction and under the railway bridge onto Barry Avenue. Pick up the pavement cycle way before picking up the road cycle lane which heads along Thames Avenue and over Windsor Br. Immediately over the bridge go L onto Brocas Street, bearing R to become Meadow Lane. Out of Eton head off the tarmac surface at the R-hand bend and onto a track to meet the railway bridge. Don't go under the bridge but head onto the track alongside the arches to reach the B3026 where you go L. Coming into Eton Wick head L onto the bridleway track opposite the church. The main track will shortly be resurfaced to come alongside the Thames towpath then onto a minor road. Head R up this road, through Boveney, and meet the B3026 again. Head L into Dorney and take the first L signed for Dorney Reach. At the R-hand bend past Dorney Court head L off the road and pick up a track to the R of the road to the quarry. Follow this over the aggregate conveyor belt to cross Summerleaze Bridge. Continue on the track to a T-junction and R.

Quiet reflection on the Thames near Kingston Bridge (section 1)

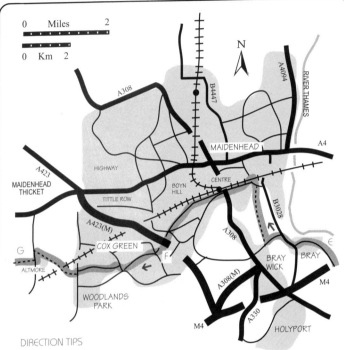

DIRECTION TIPS

E - F Continue away from Summerleaze Bridge as the track becomes tarmac and enters Bray. Bear L onto Ferry Rd. then R onto the main village road, in front of the post office. Out of Bray go first L down Hibbert Rd. Entering Bray Wick go R off the road just before Winbury School onto a woodland track and jink R then L onto the well-surfaced Green Way. Head L down the side of the next stream and emerge onto a road by a millennium marker post. Jink L then R onto Depot Rd. and bend L onto a path behind a car park (currently you must dismount on this section). Emerge at the dual carriageway and head straight over it onto Shoppenhangers Lane (small detour under rail bridge necessary). First R onto Ludlow Rd then pick up the pavement cycle track on your R, staying parallel to the railway on the R. Meet Brunel Rd and descend to the R to pick up a path at the bottom. In about 20m turn L to cross a road and R onto the path through a small estate park. Out of the park go L onto Desborough Crescent and L on meeting the main road. Bend L onto Norris Drive onto the shared cycleway. About 30m after Norton Rd head R onto the path which follows a subway under the A423 motorway.

F - G Emerge at the road after the subway and go L onto the shared cycle path. By the Foresters pub go R down Cox Green Lane. At the T-junction with Highfield Avenue jink R then L onto a short cycle path to emerge in a new housing area. Head around the R-hand side of the small green playground area and follow a short section of cycle path and onto yet another estate road. At the end of Gatward Avenue go R then immediate L. At the end of Loosen Drive go R and follow Lowbrook Drive on Bissley Drive. Follow Bissley Drive to the main road where you go L then first R up Breadcroft Lane (marked dead end) which leaves the Woodland Park estate to become a rural track. Follow the track over a railway and to the minor road in Altmore and go L. In about 70m go R onto an off-road track (marked as a footpath at time of writing but due to be upgraded after negotiation).

NOTE Between here and Knowl Hill the track surface may be very muddy in winter or after rain. If you feel you want to avoid this you can go R on meeting the road in Altmore, not L. On meeting the A4 (BUSY & FAST) go L towards Wargrave. Finally pick up the B477 to Wargrave.

The off-road surface of the 'official' route is due to be resurfaced and improved by Sustrans although exactly when is uncertain.

The ferry at Shepperton (section 1)

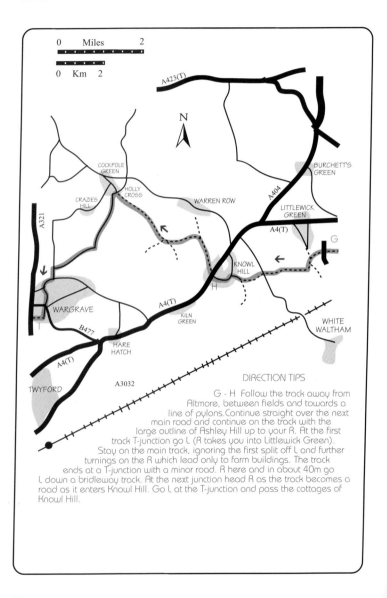

DIRECTION TIPS

G - H Follow the track away from
Altmore, between fields and towards a
line of pylons. Continue straight over the next
main road and continue on the track with the
large outline of Ashley Hill up to your R. At the first
track T-junction go L (R takes you into Littlewick Green).
Stay on the main track, ignoring the first split off L and further
turnings on the R which lead only to farm buildings. The track
ends at a T-junction with a minor road. R here and in about 40m go
L down a bridleway track. At the next junction head R as the track becomes a
road as it enters Knowl Hill. Go L at the T-junction and pass the cottages of
Knowl Hill.

H - I Meet the main road in Knowl Hill and jink R then L up Star Lane. Ignore the first L to the quarry and continue through a small housing area and begin to climb on this track. After a stiff climb the track narrows to a footpath and you strike off L, continuing to climb on the wider bridleway. As the climb levels out come to a major track junction and take the R-hand most option. Pass Bowsey Manor on the L. Descend to meet the road at Holly Cross and L. Descend for over a mile to a T-junction and L. After going R at the next T-junction, take the next L down Dark Lane then L onto School Hill. Take the first R down Braybrooke Rd. Follow the road nearly to the end but before it emerges onto open fields go R down a track between houses (opposite a footpath). Emerge at the A321 and L.

The bridge at Wallingford (section 3)

3 WARGRAVE - WALLINGFORD

Section Distance 23 miles / 37 km   **Off-road** 7 miles / 11 km

The Route This a section of two distinct halves. From Wargrave to Reading the twentieth century is very much in evidence, with plenty of cyclepaths alongside dual carriageways before the predominantly industrial character of Reading takes over. As you climb up and out of Reading, however, the Chilterns scenery just seems to get better and better as you pass through mature woodland before the long downhill descent towards Wallingford. Although there are some moderate climbs up onto the Chilterns the quiet minor roads used make this a relatively easy task.

WARGRAVE TO READING

• **Sonning's** village centre, right next to the route, is well worth a look. Amongst many charming buildings are the restored church, The Deanery and **Bull Inn**. There is also a handy tea room. An important parish centre in Saxon times and seat of the Bishop of Salisbury. Although busy at weekends with visitors Sonning is now essentially a quiet residential village.

WARGRAVE TO READING - ACCOMMODATION

Chesam House, 79 Wargrave Road, Twyford (0118) 9320428
The Thatched Cottage, Park View Drive North, Charvil (0118) 9340133

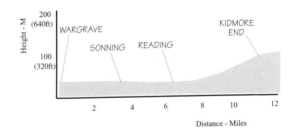

40

READING - HISTORY AND ATTRACTIONS

• Although Reading today seems dominated by industry, housing and traffic it does have its interesting corners. In the 19th century it was known for the production of the **three 'b's - beer, bulbs and biscuits.**
• **The Buttermarket** is a real mix of architecture. The unusual looking St. Laurence's Church houses a monument to a mathematician. Surrounding the church are timber-framed house, Georgian house and the old Corn Exchange.
• In **Forbury Gardens** stands the Maiwand Lion, commemorating men who died in the Afghan campaign. Nearby are the Abbey Gatehouse and ruins.
• **Blake's Lock Museum** is on the Kennet and Avon Canal which runs through Reading centre. 19th and 20th century Reading life housed in Victorian buildings. Displays on local industries and waterways life. Free admission. (0118) 9390918.
• **Museum of English Rural Life** Reading University White Knights Campus. (0118) 9318660

READING - ACCOMMODATION

Adair, 46 Redlands Road (0118) 9863792. £££££-SEC.
Thames House Hotel, 18-19 Thameside (0118) 9507951. £££/£-DR-LAU-SEC. On the route, 10 mins from Reading centre.
Beechdale Guest House, 6 Western Elms Avenue (0118) 9574074
Berkeley Guest House, 32 Berkeley Avenue (0118) 9595699
Crescent Hotel, 35 Coley Avenue (0118) 9507980
The Gorge Cafe, 227 Caversham Road (0118) 9571449
Orchid Bed and Breakfast, 1 Micklands Road, Caversham (0118) 9479635

READING - OTHER INFORMATION

Tourist Information Town Hall, Blagrave Street (0118) 9566226
Hospital A&E at Royal Berkshire Hospital, Craven Rd. (0118) 9875111
Banks All major branches (cashpoints) on High St., Mkt. Pl. and Broad St.
    Freewheel 44 West St. (0118) 9510949. Berkshire Bicycle Co., 20 Wokingham Rd. (0118) 9661799. Cycology Cycles, 186 Loddon Bridge Rd., Woodley (0118) 9695776.

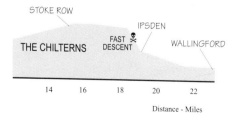

Distance - Miles

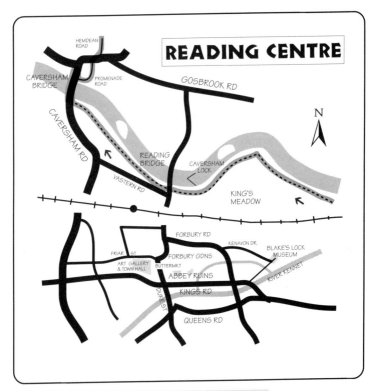

READING TO WALLINGFORD - ACCOMMODATION

Little Gables, 166 Crowmarsh Hill, Crowmarsh Gifford (01491) 837834. ££££/
£-PL-DR-SEC-WKSH.
52 Blackstone Road, Wallingford (01491) 839339. ££/£-DR-SEC-WKSH.
Squires Guest House, 9a St. Johns Rd., Wallingford (01491) 837707
Munts Mill, Castle Lane, Wallingford (01491) 836654
The Nook, Thames Street, Wallingford (01491) 834214
The Studio, 85 Wantage Road, Wallingford (01491) 837277
The Dolphin, 2 St Mary's St., Wallingford (01491) 837377
Homelea Guest House, 83 Wantage Rd., Wallingford (01491) 825549
△ **Bridge Villa International Camping**, Crowmarsh Gifford (01491) 836860.
March - Oct. **Riverside Park**, Wallingford (01491) 835232. May - Sept.

READING TO WALLINGFORD

• After a steepish climb to Tanners Lane comes the pretty village of **Kidmore End**, with the **New Inn** and its upmarket menu. **Reformation** pub in Gallowstree Common.

• As on the more northerly return leg, **beechwood** is very much in evidence whilst crossing the **Chilterns**. Unlike section 6 the climbing is gentle however.

• The main feature of **Stoke Row** is the **Maharajah's Well.** This was donated by the Maharajah of Benares and its 368 foot depth supplied local people with water until 1939. Deeper than St. Paul's is high, it was dug entirely by hand. Next door is the pretty Cherry Orchard, also given by the Maharajah. **Cherry Tree Pub. Black Horse Pub** on route just out of Stoke Row.

• **Wallingford** is a fine Thames-side town. Fire destroyed most of the medieval town but many 17th and 18th century buildings remain around the market square. The main features are:

• **The Castle** Once important in medieval times (the Treaty of Wallingford ending the civil war between Stephen and Matilda was signed here) it was destroyed by Cromwell in reaction to royalist resistance here. The remains, in an enclosed park area are worth a look. The most significant building left standing is the tower of the 16th century St. Nicholas' Church

• Portions of **pre-medieval earthworks** in the Kine Croft Recreation Ground show the town was an important enough site to defend even before the Normans.

• The elegant hollow spire you see on entering the town is that of **St. Peters**. The famous Judge Blackstone (author of *Commentaries on the Laws of England*) is buried here, which is quite fitting as he actually paid for the church.

• **St. Leonard's** is an attractive church in a beautiful corner of the town.

• The seventeenth century **Town Hall** dominates the market square. Tourist information office is found here (01491) 826972

• **Wallingford Bridge** is a graceful 900 feet long and provides a spectacular entrance to the town.

• **Wallingford Museum** is housed in part of a medieval hall and takes you through the ages in Wallingford. (01491) 835065

WALLINGFORD - OTHER INFORMATION

Tourist Information Town Hall, Market Place (01491) 826972
Hospital Wallingford Community Hospital, Reading Road (01491) 835533
Banks Natwest on High Street, Lloyds and Barclays on the market square and a Link machine on St. Mary's Street.
ڶڶ Rides On Air, 45 St. Mary's St. (01491) 836289.

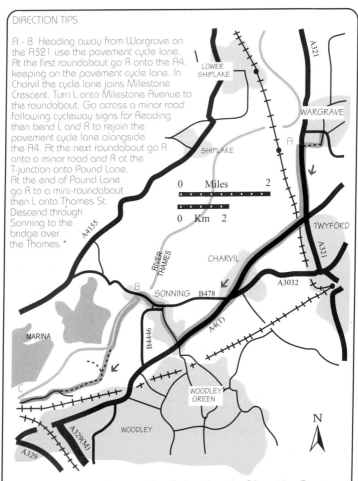

DIRECTION TIPS

A - B Heading away from Wargrave on the A321 use the pavement cycle lane. At the first roundabout go R onto the A4, keeping on the pavement cycle lane. In Charvil the cycle lane joins Milestone Crescent. Turn L onto Milestone Avenue to the roundabout. Go across a minor road following cycleway signs for Reading then bend L and R to rejoin the pavement cycle lane alongside the A4. At the next roundabout go R onto a minor road and R at the T-junction onto Pound Lane. At the end of Pound Lane go R to a mini-roundabout then L onto Thames St. Descend through Sonning to the bridge over the Thames.*

* The official signed route will go further along the A4 avoiding Sonning. You may wish to follow the official signs but the route shown here is nicer and entirely legal.

WARGRAVE - WALLINGFORD

44

B - C Just before Sonning Bridge go L onto the Thames Path, keeping the Thames on your R. Pass Sonning Lock (dismount). Leave the towpath by the Millennium Milepost (Reading 2, Sonning 1), heading L up a good track. Bear L to stay on the main track by the small pond. At the next track T-junction go L, coming alongside office and light industrial development. At the end of the track head through a small car park and onto the pavement cycle lane at the side of a dual carriageway. Now in Thames Valley Business Park, follow the cycle lane to a car park just before the next roundabout. Head R, through the car park and across the grass to rejoin the Thames-side path. NOTE - there will be a sports centre here within the next 12 months but there will be cycle access through it to get alongside the Thames.

D'Oyly Carte Island near Shepperton (section 1)

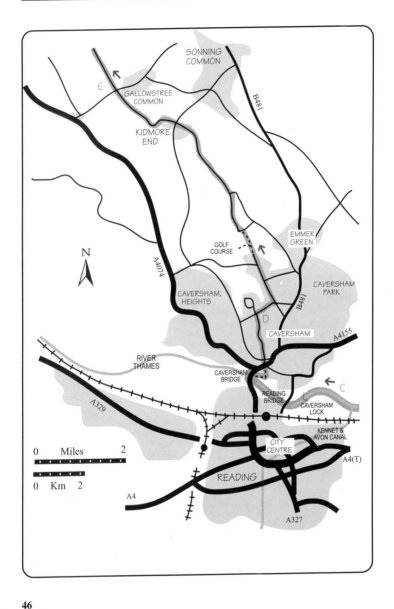

DIRECTION TIPS

C - D Continue on the Thames-side path past the gas towers on the L. Pass over a bridge across the Kennet and Avon Canal where it joins the Thames and continue by the river on your R. After passing through King's Meadow park area the track becomes tarmac alongside Caversham Lock. Simply follow the riverside, on a variety of paths, under Reading Bridge until meeting Caversham Bridge. Immediately after crossing over Caversham Bridge take the first R down Promenade Rd and L up the tarmac path in front of Christchurch Meadows. Follow the path through a housing development to emerge on the busy Church Street. Head R then immediate L up Hemdean Road. (NOTE - The route may go through a small park area to the R of Hemdean Road at some future date; this is currently under negotiation).

D - E Follow the road to the first junction and R onto Rotherfield Way. Go next L up Surley Row. Turn L in front of Highdown School (ignoring Grove Road to the R) and straight on at the next roundabout, passing Old Barn Close on the R. Stay on this road as it narrows and descends to become unmetalled. At a fork in the track bear R to cross over a golf course then begin a short but steepish ascent which ends at a minor road. L onto the road and shortly pass Kidmore Pheasant Farm. At the end of Tanners Lane come to a T-junction and go L, in glorious open countryside. Stay on this road through Kidmore End and at the first staggered crossroads after Kidmore End go R then L signed for Stoke Row (Gallowstree Common to the R).

The market square in Wallingford (section 3 / 4)

DIRECTION TIPS

E - F Heading away from the Gallowstree Common junction cross over the first crossroads. Continue through glorious beechwoods for just under 2 miles, ignoring the only L turn, to come to a crossroads in Stoke Row. Go L onto the main road through the village, passing Maharajah's Well on the R. Take the first L just leaving Stoke Row down Uxmore Rd, towards Checkendon. In 300-400m take the first unsigned R (easy to miss) and very shortly come to a T-junction and R. Pass the Black Horse pub on this very minor road and head back into forest. Go straight over the next crossroads. Take the next L signed for Ipsden. This leads out of the woods to a superb viewpoint over south-east Oxfordshire.

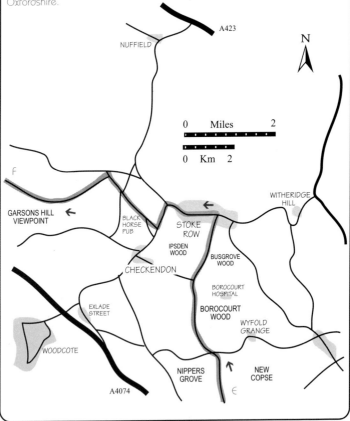

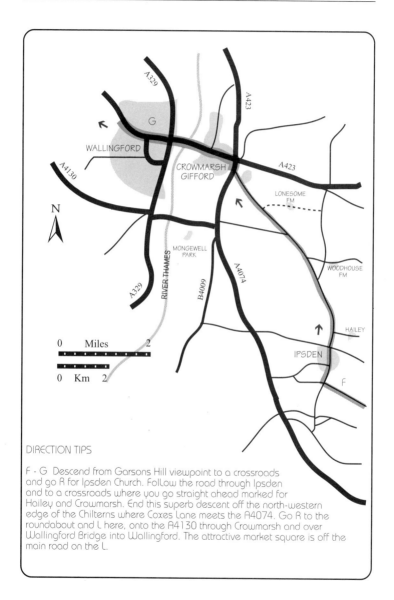

DIRECTION TIPS

F - G Descend from Garsons Hill viewpoint to a crossroads
and go R for Ipsden Church. Follow the road through Ipsden
and to a crossroads where you go straight ahead marked for
Hailey and Crowmarsh. End this superb descent off the north-western
edge of the Chilterns where Coxes Lane meets the A4074. Go R to the
roundabout and L here, onto the A4130 through Crowmarsh and over
Wallingford Bridge into Wallingford. The attractive market square is off the
main road on the L.

4 WALLINGFORD - OXFORD

Section Distance 22 miles / 35 km   **Off-road** 7.5 miles / 12 km

The Route South-east Oxfordshire is largely flat and undeveloped with many beautifully preserved villages such as Brightwell-cum-Sotwell, Long Wittenham and Sutton Courtenay. The occasional eyesore, such as the dominant power station neat Didcot, is the exception that proves the rule. The fine view from the Wittenham Clumps gives a good overview of the undemanding topography that lies ahead of you. The route outline here is very much an interim route. There remain large off-road sections of the route to be completed, including a section between Appleford and Sutton Courtenay and another from east of Abingdon to Donnington Bridge, south of Oxford.

WALLINGFORD TO ABINGDON

• **Brightwell-cum-Sotwell** Beautiful village with interesting restored churches. **Red Lion** pub.
• **Wittenham Clumps** The route passes in front of these beech-clad hills but there are even more magnificent views if you have the energy to lock your bike in the car park and climb to the top. Fine views over the Thames Valley to the north and beyond Didcot onto the Downs to the south. Earthworks of the Iron-Age Sinodoun Camp also remain here.
• **Long Wittenham** As the name suggests, this pretty village straggles along the main street. Village boasts ancient church, St. Anthony's Well, Saxon cross, a cruck cottage, fishponds and a pigeon cote. **Pendon Museum**, passed as you exit the village, has countryside and railway models. Aims to recreate the English countryside of the 1930s. Admission charge. (01865) 407365 **Machine Man Inn** Meals 12-2 & 6.30-9.30. Wide range of food. Summer Lightening, Wychwood, Abbot Ale & Skiff ales. Also **Vine** and **Plough** pubs.

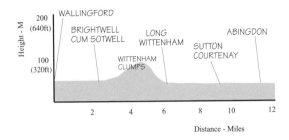

• **Sutton Courtenay** Enchanting village, filled with trees, grass and half-timbered houses. Norman manor house and 14th century abbey building. In the churchyard look out for the graves of Asquith (former prime minister), Eric Blair (author George Orwell) and Mrs Martha Pye who died in 1822 aged 117.

WALLINGFORD TO ABINGDON - ACCOMMODATION

White Cottage, Brightwell-cum-Sotwell (01491) 837020
Small's House, Macney, Brightwell-cum-Sotwell (01491) 839167
Rooks Orchard, Little Wittenham (01865) 407765
Machine Man Inn, Long Wittenham (01865) 407835. ££££/£-DR.
Wittas Ham Cottage, High St., Long Wittenham (01865) 407686
Bekynton House, 7 The Green, Sutton Courtenay (01235) 848630
⛺ **Day's Lock**, Little Wittenham (01867) 307768. Idyllic camping on river island but without facilities!

ABINGDON

• Historic riverside **market town**, centred around the market place. Once the capital of Berkshire it now lies firmly in south-east Oxfordshire. Beautiful vistas of the town from the banks of the Thames. Numerous interesting buildings include County Hall and numerous almshouses. For full details see map overleaf.
• **Abingdon Museum**, located in the upper storey of County Hall, houses displays on local history, arts and crafts. Free admission. (01235) 523703.

ABINGDON - ACCOMMODATION

22 East St Helen's St (01235) 550979. £££££-PL-DR-SEC.
Pastures Green, 46 Picklers Hill (01235) 521369. £££-DR-LAU-SEC-Tools.
Oxford Guest House, 37 Oxford Road (01235) 520151
14 Andersey Road (01235) 520060
Caroline's Cottage, 50 West St. Helen's Street (01235) 202873
Conifers, 5 Galleyfields, Radley Road (01235) 521088

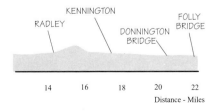

KENNINGTON

RADLEY

FOLLY BRIDGE

DONNINGTON BRIDGE

| 14 | 16 | 18 | 20 | 22 |

Distance - Miles

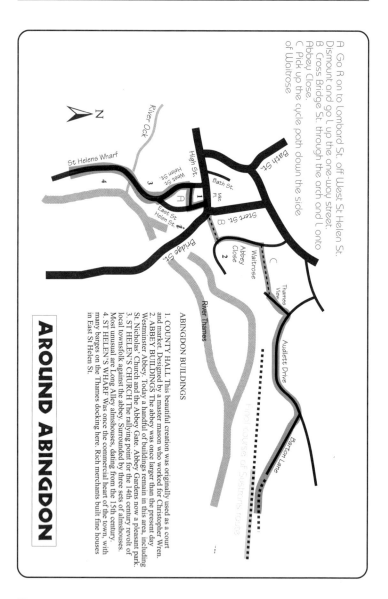

AROUND ABINGDON

A Go R on to Lombard St. off West St Helen St.
Dismount and go L up the one-way street.
B Cross Bridge St. through the arch and L onto
Abbey Close.
C Pick up the cycle path down the side
of Waitrose

ABINGDON BUILDINGS

1. COUNTY HALL. This beautiful creation was originally used as a court
and market. Designed by a master mason who worked for Christopher Wren.
2. ABBEY BUILDINGS The abbey was once larger than the present day
Westminster Abbey. Today a handful of buildings remain in this area, including
St. Nicholas' Church and the Abbey Gate. Abbey Gardens now a pleasant park.
3. ST HELEN'S CHURCH The rallying point for the 14th century revolt of
local townsfolk against the abbey. Surrounded by three sets of almshouses.
Most unusual are Long Alley almshouses, dating from the 15th century.
4. ST HELEN'S WHARF Was once the commercial heart of the town, with
many barges on the Thames docking here. Rich merchants built fine houses
in East St Helen St.

ABINGDON - OTHER INFORMATION

Tourist Information 25 Bridge Street (01235) 522711
Hospital No A&E hospital - the nearest is the John Radcliffe in Oxford (pg 56)
Banks Natwest, Market Place; Barclays, The Square; Link (Nationwide), High Street; Lloyds, Ock St; Midland with cashpoint on High St.
 ⮌   Abingdon Pedal Power, 92 The Vineyard, Oxford Rd. (01235) 525123. Above Board and Behind Bars, Ock St. (01235) 535624. Braggs Bicycles, 2 High St. (01235) 520034.

ABINGDON TO OXFORD

• **Radley** is home to the famous college which lies next to a pretty village of timbered houses, an attractive old rectory and a church.
• The final route of the Thames Valley Cycle Route into Oxford will avoid the rather nondescript Kennington by running parallel to the railway line. **The Thames** is rejoined at **Donnington Bridge** and from here to **Folly Bridge** quieter riverside scenery predominates. You may see **eights** or single **sculls** rowing on this stretch, most probably from one of the college boathouses. You get a good view of the eastern bank, passing **Iffley Fields, college boathouses** and **Christ Church Meadows**. The latter are backed impressively by Christ Church, Corpus Christi and Merton Colleges. The official Sustrans route will use the western side of the A4144. You can follow their signs but the alternative route along the Thames path given here is picturesque and legal!

OXFORD

• One of the grandest cities in England, dominated by the **University**, and standing on the confluence of the Thames (called the Isis here) and the Cherwell. The University was never officially founded but evolved into today's myriad of colleges. Scholars were active here in the 12th century and the subsequent relationship between 'town and gown' was often stormy. There were several violent incidents but gown eventually gained the ascendancy over town with the University Chancellor acquiring greater powers and, following an economic downturn, the University was able to acquire much of central Oxford. In the 17th century it became the Royalist capital during the Civil War and Magdalen and New Colleges were made into arsenals. The town was successfully besieged in 1646. Many of the finest buildings were constructed in the eighteenth century including the Radcliffe Camera and the Clarendon Building. The nineteenth century saw the modern examination system introduced and the University became a production line creating the professional elite who ran the Empire. You can spend several days in Oxford exploring this rich and fascinating historical legacy. A small selection of the main attractions is shown on the map overleaf.

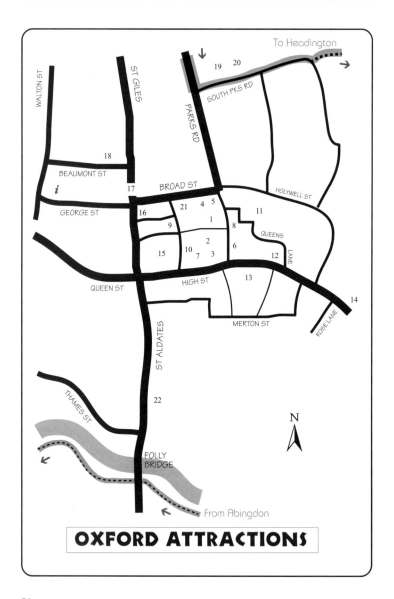

OXFORD ATTRACTIONS

KEY TO MAP * Indicates open to the public. No indication is given for the colleges. The majority are open to the public but they may close without notice.

1. **Bodleian Library** One of the greatest libraries in the world with several million books. Superb architecture dating from the 17th century, especially in Schools Quadrangle. * Selected parts.
2. **Radcliffe Camera** Circular 18th century addition to the Bodleian, sits magnificently between Brasenose and All Souls in a beautiful square.
3. **University Church of St. Mary the Virgin** Early centre of university ceremony and administration. Has the oldest surviving library room in Britain. *
4. **Sheldonian Theatre** The ceremonial hall of the University. Designed by Christopher Wren in an unusual D-shape with cupola roof. Ceiling painted as an open sky.
5. **Clarendon Building** Originally designed as a purpose-built 'production plant' for the famous Oxford University Press, it is now used mainly for meetings.
6. **All Souls College** Elite graduate college for the cream of the academic world. Look out for the Codrington Library with many priceless texts and a beautiful concert venue. All Souls is the home of the bizarre Mallard ceremony (performed once a century), when a dead duck is carried onto the rooftop!
7. **Brasenose College** Named after the college's door-knocker which features a large brass nose! The knocker now hangs above High Table.
8. **Hertford College** Famous for the 'Bridge of Sighs' on New College Lane.
9. **Jesus College** The 'Welshman's college' with fine 17th century buildings.
10. **Lincoln College** Medieval buildings. Former All Saints Church now its library.
11. **New College** Cloister and bell tower famous for gargoyles.
12. **Queens College** Classical style buildings and a beautiful library.
13. **University College** Memorial to Shelley (a former pupil) and varied quads.
14. **Magdalen College** Bell tower is a well-known landmark and centre of the 'May Morning' celebrations. Highlights include Cloister Quad with hieroglyph monsters and New Buildings. The latter lead to the beautiful Magdalen Meadows.
15. **Covered Market** Full of character with excellent cafes! *
16. **Saxon Tower** Oxford's oldest building, and once an important lookout.
17. **Martyrs Memorial** to protestant Bishops, burnt as heretics by Mary Tudor.
18. **Ashmolean Museum** Superb displays of European and Eastern antiquities, European paintings, Oriental art and more. Admission free. (01865) 278000*
19. **Museum of Natural History** Includes some offbeat displays in a superb Victorian Gothic building. Free admission. (01865) 272950.*
20. **Pitt Rivers Museum** Strange and beautiful anthropological and archaeological displays. Free admission. (01865) 270927*
21. **Museum of History of Science** Science dating from antiquity. Free admission. (01865) 277280.*
22. **Christ Church** Tom Tower houses Great Tom Bell. One of the grandest Oxford colleges.

OXFORD - ACCOMMODATION

Arden Lodge, 34 Sunderland Avenue (01865) 552076. ££££/£-DR-SEC.
11 Polstead Rd (01865) 556971. £££ and up-PL-DR-SEC-WKSH.
Falcon Private Hotel, 88-90 Abingdon Rd (01865) 722995. ££££/£-PL-DR-LAU-SEC-Tools.
High Hedges, 8 Cumnor Hill (01865) 863395. ££££-PL-DR-LAU-SEC.
Acorn Guest House, 260-262 Iffley Rd (01865) 247998. £££/£-DR-SEC.
Oxford Backpackers' Hostel, 9A Hythe Bridge Street (01865) 721761. ££-DR-LAU-SEC.
Youth Hostel, 32 Jack Straw's Lane (01865) 762997. ££-SEC-LAU.
Newton House, 82-84 Abingdon Road (01865) 240561
Sportsview Guesthouse, 106-110 Abingdon Road (01865) 244268
Whitehouse View, 9 Whitehouse Road (01865) 721626
　△ **Salter Bros Caravan Site**, Slipway Meadow Lane, Donnington Bridge (01865) 243421. **Oxford Camping International**, 426 Abingdon Rd. (01865) 244088. May to Sept.

OXFORD - OTHER INFORMATION

Tourist Information The Old School, Gloucester Green (01865) 726871
Hospital John Radcliffe Infirmary, Headley Way, Headington (01865) 741166
Banks All major branches on High Street and Cornmarket St. with cashpoints. (Lloyds on Broad St.)
　🚲 Reg Taylor Cycles, 285 Iffley Rd. (01865) 247040. Bee-Line Cycles, 61-63 Cowley Rd. (01865) 246615. Bike Zone, 5-6 Market St. (01865) 728877. Botley Road Cycles, 63 Botley Rd. (01865) 723100. Cycle King, 56 Walton St. (01865) 516122. Cyclo Analysts, 150 Cowley Rd. (01865) 424444.

The Thames Valley Cycle Route enters Abingdon by the Thames

CLASSIC THAMES LANDSCAPES

Above: Houseboats at Molesey (section 1)
Below: Pomp and circumstance near Richmond Bridge (section 8)

Above: The green Thame, a tributary of the Thames (section 5)
Below: Rowing on the Thames at Abingdon (section 4)

<u>CLASSIC BIKING</u>

Above: Summerleaze Bridge (section 2)   Below: Ferry near Ham House (section 8)
Previous page: Delightful footbridge near the route at Teddington Locks (section 1)

Above: Autumn colour by Maidenhead Bridge (section 2)
Below: Never too young to cycle! Richmond Park (sections 1 & 8)

CLASSIC GRAND UNION CANAL

Above: Quiet towpath near Cassiobury Park (section 7)
Below: Boatyard near Southall (section 8)

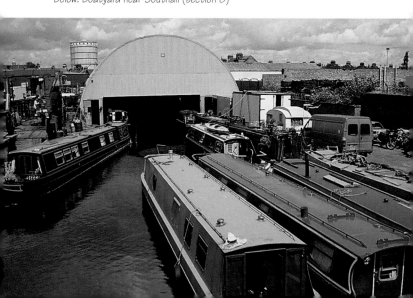

<u>CLASSIC TRACKS</u>

Above: Approaching Appleford (section 4)
Below: Bowsey Hill (section 2)

CLASSIC BUILDINGS

Left: Ham House (section 8)
Below: Typical south-east Oxfordshire thatching (section 5)

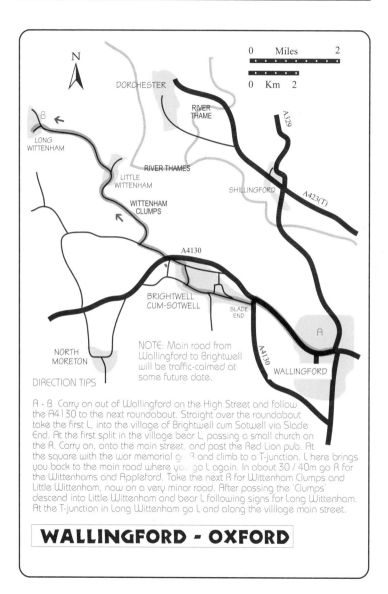

N

DORCHESTER

RIVER THAME

B ←

LONG WITTENHAM

A329

RIVER THAMES

LITTLE WITTENHAM

SHILLINGFORD

A423(T)

WITTENHAM CLUMPS

←

A4130

BRIGHTWELL CUM-SOTWELL

SLADE END

A

NORTH MORETON

A4130

WALLINGFORD

NOTE: Main road from Wallingford to Brightwell will be traffic-calmed at some future date.

DIRECTION TIPS

0   Miles   2

0   Km   2

A - B Carry on out of Wallingford on the High Street and follow the A4130 to the next roundabout. Straight over the roundabout take the first L, into the village of Brightwell cum Sotwell via Slade End. At the first split in the village bear L, passing a small church on the R. Carry on, onto the main street, and past the Red Lion pub. At the square with the war memorial go R and climb to a T-junction. L here brings you back to the main road where you go L again. In about 30 / 40m go R for the Wittenhams and Appleford. Take the next R for Wittenham Clumps and Little Wittenham, now on a very minor road. After passing the 'Clumps' descend into Little Wittenham and bear L following signs for Long Wittenham. At the T-junction in Long Wittenham go L and along the village main street.

WALLINGFORD - OXFORD

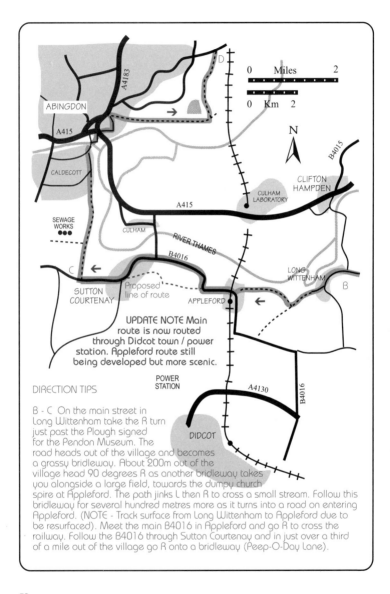

0 Miles 2

0 Km 2

N

ABINGDON

A4183

A415

CALDECOTT

SEWAGE
WORKS
●●●

CULHAM

D

→

CLIFTON
HAMPDEN

B4015

A415

CULHAM
LABORATORY

RIVER THAMES

B4016

C ←

SUTTON
COURTENAY

Proposed
line of route

APPLEFORD

LONG
WITTENHAM

B

←

UPDATE NOTE Main
route is now routed
through Didcot town / power
station. Appleford route still
being developed but more scenic.

DIRECTION TIPS

B - C On the main street in
Long Wittenham take the R turn
just past the Plough signed
for the Pendon Museum. The
road heads out of the village and becomes
a grassy bridleway. About 200m out of the
village head 90 degrees R as another bridleway takes
you alongside a large field, towards the dumpy church
spire at Appleford. The path jinks L then R to cross a small stream. Follow this
bridleway for several hundred metres more as it turns into a road on entering
Appleford. (NOTE - Track surface from Long Wittenham to Appleford due to
be resurfaced). Meet the main B4016 in Appleford and go R to cross the
railway. Follow the B4016 through Sutton Courtenay and in just over a third
of a mile out of the village go R onto a bridleway (Peep-O-Day Lane).

POWER
STATION

A4130

B4016

DIDCOT

DIRECTION TIPS

C - D Follow the well-surfaced Peep-O-Day Lane and continue on past Thames Water sewage works on your L. Follow the track to come to a T-junction on a housing estate and go R. Head onto North Quay and from here pick up the small link on the L, passing Andersey Way on the L and onto Wilsham Road which comes alongside the Thames on your R. At the next junction, coming into central Abingdon, go R to pass over the River Ock and onto St. Helen's Wharf. For directions through Abingdon to the start of the off-road section towards Radley see map on page 52. Once you have found the track* stay on it for about 2 miles, until you head L** onto a track on your L, with water now on both sides of you (reservoir on your R is banked and fenced off). Follow this track to a T-junction with a minor road. Go R and follow Thrupp Lane to its end.

* NOTE: The whole of the following track section was in very poor condition at the time of writing and had several stiles and 'No Right of Way' signs on it but it may well have been resurfaced by the time you do the route. If still unimproved and you find it too difficult you may want to continue on Barton Lane which is bridleway and runs roughly parallel with the actual route to emerge at the point marked** in the above directions.

The tranquil looking Thames at Abingdon Bridge (section 4)

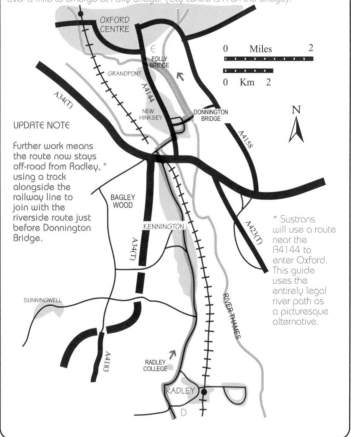

DIRECTION TIPS

D - E At the junction at the end of Thrupp Lane jink R then L onto Whites Lane. Follow this road and descend into Kennington with views of Oxford ahead of you. Through the modern development of Kennington pass under a flyover to a T-junction and R. Over the railway bridge bear L at the major road junction and cross over at the first pelican crossing to head R down Canning Crescent. At the next T-junction go R onto the cycle lane. Cross over one bridge and at the next head L down to the Thames-side path. Follow the river on your R for just over a mile to emerge at Folly Bridge. (City centre is R on the bridge).

UPDATE NOTE

Further work means the route now stays off-road from Radley, * using a track alongside the railway line to join with the riverside route just before Donnington Bridge.

* Sustrans will use a route near the A4144 to enter Oxford. This guide uses the entirely legal river path as a picturesque alternative.

OXFORD CENTRE

E FOLLY BRIDGE

GRANDPONT

A4144

A34(T)

NEW HINKSEY

DONNINGTON BRIDGE

A4158

0 Miles 2

0 Km 2

N

BAGLEY WOOD

KENNINGTON

A34(T)

A423(T)

SUNNINGWELL

RIVER THAMES

A4183

RADLEY COLLEGE

RADLEY

D

60

The main entrance to the grand Christ Church College (section 4/5)

5 OXFORD - PRINCES RISBOROUGH

Section Distance 27 miles / 43 km   **Off-road** 7 miles / 11km

The Route After starting at Folly Bridge in Oxford an off-road adventure to see the non-tourist Oxford of the canal, impressive residences and the University Parks awaits you (although there are plenty of bikes in Oxford centre there is also plenty of motor traffic so you are best to 'park up' and explore on foot). Out of Oxford and across the impressive views of Shotover Plain the route flattens to pass through perfect thatched villages such as Waterperry before entering the market town of Thame, with its impressive array of architecture. A newly created off-road path then leads through more scenic villages to Princes Risborough at the base of the Chilterns.

OXFORD TO THAME

• The route around Oxford shows another side of the city, away from the tourist hordes. **Osney Lock** is near the site of the 12th century **Osney Abbey**. Taken apart during the Reformation, the best way to picture what was there is to look at the glass window of the abbey in Christ Church Cathedral. **Port Meadow** is the huge area of pasture to the north, visible from Weir Cottage, grazed by a variety of animals and occasionally flooded.
• **Headington** Seemingly just a suburb of Oxford but in fact the result of several small villages joining together. On the main road look out for the polytechnic (Oxford Brookes University) and Oxford United's ground. On New High St. in New Headington look out for the shark in the roof!
Banks All major banks on main London Road through Headington.
 歮 G.H.Williams, 115 London Rd (01865) 762664. Mark Munday, 4d New High St. (01865) 308757.

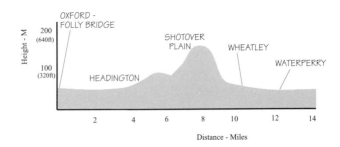

Headington Quarry provided stone to build many Oxford colleges.

• **Shotover Plain** Fine views from the rough track over this country park. Once housed the old London Road and was part of a royal hunting forest.

• **Wheatley** Pretty stone village with unusual pyramidal stone lock-up. Old windmill on Windmill Lane. Handy services include shop, toilets and Barclays Bank with cashpoint.

• **Waterperry** The **gardens** here surround a manor house (now a horticultural training college) and a church which contains many reminders of successive local aristocrats, the Fitzelys, Curzons and Henleys. Restored barn and tearoom. (01844) 339254 for details.

• **Waterstock** Beautiful thatched village with horse stables and many 'dream' houses. Church contains the tomb of judge George Croke whose refusal of ship money contributed to the outbreak of the Civil War.

• **Long Crendon** National Trust **Court House**. Originally a wool store then manorial courts from the reign of Henry V onwards. April - Sept. Wednesday afternoons, weekends and bank holidays. Small admission fee. Other impressive buildings include Long Crendon Manor and the church with Dormer tomb.

OXFORD TO THAME - ACCOMMODATION

Holbeach, Worminghall Road, Waterperry (01844) 339623. £££/£-PL-DR-LAU-SEC-WKSH. Dinner plus 'quick' menu. Closed Jan & Feb except for booking well in advance.

Common Leys Farm, Waterperry Common (01865) 351266 / (0802) 960651 ££££-PL-DR-LAU-SEC. About 1.5 miles to the north of the route at Waterperry.

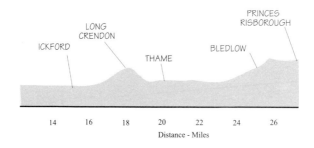

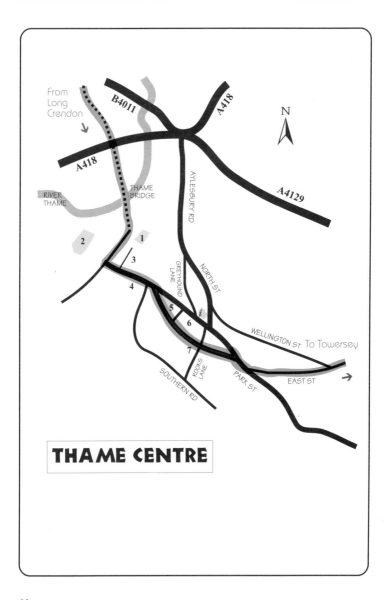

THAME CENTRE

THAME - HISTORY AND ATTRACTIONS

• Elegant and stylish **market town** established in medieval times by the Bishop of Lincoln. Important Parliamentary centre in the Civil War, used as a base from which to attack Royalist Oxford.
• **Thame Show** combines with the Fair and claims to be the largest one-day show in England (third Thursday in September).
• Many **outstanding buildings** (shown numbered on the map opposite and listed below).

THAME - TOWN CENTRE BUILDINGS (See map opposite)

1. **Parish Church** Situated in the oldest part of town, greeting cyclists entering Thame on the old Long Crendon road. Said to be a small-scale Lincoln Cathedral.
2. **Prebendal** Originally church land, then a farmhouse, now a private dwelling. Remains of medieval refectory and chapel visible behind gatehouse.
3. **Church St.** has some fine old buildings including an Elizabethan Grammar School and former Quartermaine Almshouses which feature an iron bandstand from the Wembley Exhibition in the garden.
4. **Lower High St.** has a mix of buildings from medieval to Victorian, including buildings with crucks and thatched roofs and the Victorian Magistrates' Court.
5. Victorian **Town Hall**. On a nearby wall is a plaque commemorating John Hampden (key figure in the Civil War against Charles I) who died here from wounds received at Chalgrove Field.
6. The middle of the High St. is divided into **Cornmarket** and **Buttermarket**, with the latter placed traditionally on the cooler northern side of the street.
7. **Upper High St.** is one of the widest streets in Britain and contains **The Birdcage**, a former leper house with its current name said to come from use as a prison for the French during the Napoleonic Wars. Further up are the Pearce Memorial Gardens and the War Memorial.

THAME - ACCOMMODATION

Black Horse Hotel, 11 Cornmarket (01844) 212886
Oakfield, Thame Park Road (01844) 213709
Vine Cottage, Moreton (just south-west of Thame off the A329). (01844) 216910

THAME - OTHER INFORMATION

Tourist Information Market House, North St. (01844) 212834
Early Closing Wednesday
Market Street market on Tuesday
Hospital No local A&E. Use the John Radcliffe in Oxford (pg 56).
Banks Cashpoints for Midland, Natwest, Lloyds and Link are all on Cornmarket with a Barclays cashpoint near the Town Hall.
🚲 Thame Cycles, 69a Park St. (01844) 261520

THAME TO PRINCES RISBOROUGH

• **Towersey** Quiet village with some Tudor and Jacobean houses. **Three Horseshoes** pub.
• **Sustrans Railpath** A short but excellent section of former rail trackbed is used to link Towersey and Forty Green.
• **Bledlow** Yet another picturesque village of thatch and rural peace. Eighteenth century Manor House owned by former Foreign Secretary, Lord Carrington. Backed by Wain Hill bearing the white chalk Bledlow Cross (unknown origin). River Lyde flows through the village. **Lions of Bledlow** pub.

THAME TO PRINCES RISBOROUGH - ACCOMMODATION

Upper Green Farm, Manor Road, Towersey ((01844) 212496
Cross Lanes Guest House, Cross Lanes Cottage, Bledlow (01844) 345339

PRINCES RISBOROUGH - HISTORY AND ATTRACTIONS

• Supposedly takes its name from the **Black Prince** who had a hunting lodge in the area. Now a pleasant market town at the base of the Chilterns.
• Oldest part of the town lies around the fine **parish church**, made of flint and stone. Nearby is the Market Square and **Market House** of 1824. Small streets of half-timbered cottages lead off the Market Square.
• Next to the church is the **Manor House**. A fine 17th century brick construction, formerly belonging to the famous Rothschild banking family, now owned by the National Trust. Admission by written arrangement with the tenant. Small admission fee.

PRINCES RISBOROUGH - ACCOMMODATION

Black Prince Hotel, 86 Wycombe Road (01844) 345569
Solis Ortu, Aylesbury Rd, Askett, Princes Risborough (01844) 344175

PRINCES RISBOROUGH - OTHER INFORMATION

Tourist Information St John's House, Church St. (01844) 274795
Market Day Thursday morning
Hospital Nearest A&E at Stoke Mandeville, Mandeville Rd. (01296) 315000
Banks Natwest, Barclays and Lloyds all with cashpoints, on or near the main street.
🚲 Boltons, Duke St. (01844) 345949

The historic Birdcage pub in Thame (section 5)

DIRECTION TIPS

A - B On Folly Br. facing south go R onto Thames-side path. Keep the river on your R until you pass Osney Lock and join East Street to meet Osney Br.
B - C Cross Osney Br. and immediate L up river-side path. Just keep the river on your L until you meet Weir Cottage. Cross the bridge and head R across the meadow onto Walton Well Rd.
C - D Circle round north Oxford to University Parks entrance as follows: L onto Longworth Rd and across main road onto Leckford Rd. Cross Woodstock Rd. and down side of church then R onto Winchester Rd. R onto main Banbury Rd then L onto Parks Rd. First L onto South Parks Rd. At sharp R-hand bend leave the road and onto the cycle track down the side of University Parks.

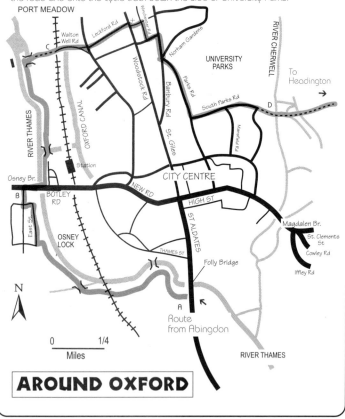

AROUND OXFORD

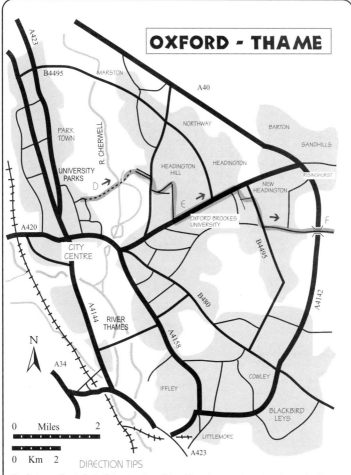

OXFORD - THAME

A423
B4495
MARSTON
A40
PARK TOWN
R. CHERWELL
NORTHWAY
BARTON
SANDHILLS
UNIVERSITY PARKS
D
HEADINGTON HILL
HEADINGTON
RISINGHURST
E
NEW HEADINGTON
A420
OXFORD BROOKES UNIVERSITY
F
CITY CENTRE
B4495
A4144
B480
A4142
RIVER THAMES
A4158
N
A34
COWLEY
IFFLEY
BLACKBIRD LEYS
0   Miles   2
LITTLEMORE
0   Km   2
A423

DIRECTION TIPS

D - E Leave South Parks Rd at the sharp R-hand bend onto cycle path to the south of University Parks. Cross river at weir. Exit track R down Ferry Rd then R onto main Marston Rd. L down John Garne Way then L at first split which becomes an uphill path. Go R onto Pullens Lane and L onto main Headington Rd. to use the cycle lane.

E - F Continue up Headington Rd. for just over 0.5 miles and R onto New High St. First L up Bateman St and R up Windmill Rd. At the end of Windmill Rd go L onto Old Rd by Rockedge Nature Reserve. Climb steeply over bypass following Shotover Plain signs.

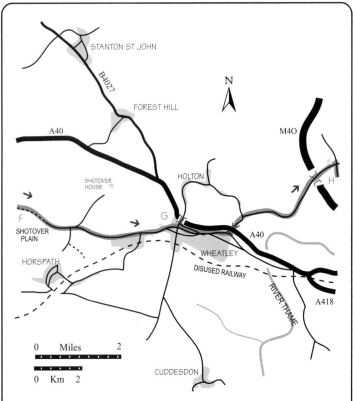

DIRECTION TIPS

F - G Climb Old Rd out of Oxford and straight on, over the rough track over Shotover Plain. Rejoin the road and descend into Wheatley to pass the unusual pyramidal lock-up on the L (town centre to your R).

G - H Meet the main road in Wheatley. R then immediate L, following signs for Waterperry. Take the next L to leave Wheatley and pass under the A40. Ignore the L for Holton. This country road leads over the M40. Take the first R after crossing the M40, signed for Waterperry.

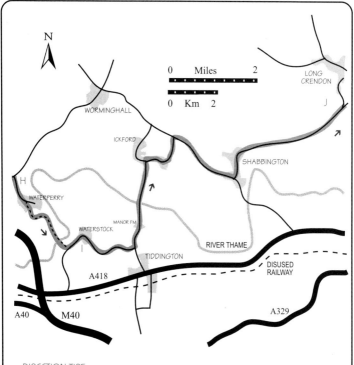

DIRECTION TIPS

H - I In Waterperry village head R off the road before Manor Farm onto a
rough track through a field, signed Oxfordshire Way Bridleway. Out
of the field jink L then R onto a better farm track, behind farm sheds. Pick up
an entrance track to Waterperry House by the fence on your L (Oxfordshire
Way picnic site is to your R here). Turn R onto the track and head away from
the house. This beautiful track leads over the River Thame and through
beautiful houses (Waterstock Mill) to a road. Go L into Waterstock village.

I - J Go L at the first T-junction out of Waterstock, for Ickford, and cross the
beautiful 'double' bridge. Enter Ickford and bear R to the main road. Go R
and into Shabbington where you take the first L, signed for Long Crendon.
Climb steadily for about 3 miles then take the first R to bring you into the
centre of Long Crendon.

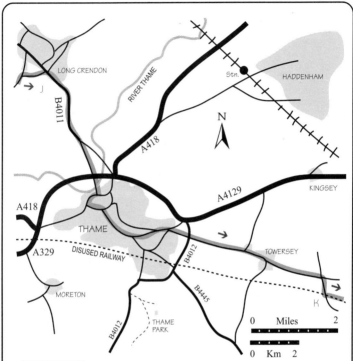

DIRECTION TIPS

J - K   Come into Long Crendon centre and go R at the crossroads on the B4011 to Thame. Approaching Thame go R onto the minor road by Thames Mead Farm (easy to miss). Pass through the bridlegate and carry on to cross the A418. Cross a bridge and emerge in front of the church to bend R. Meet the High Street and go L into Thame centre. Continue through the centre and go L onto East St in front of the Cross Keys pub. Past the hospital go R down Kings Road. L at the next junction then R down Towersey Rd. Cross the B4012 ring road and onto a minor road. In Towersey go straight over the crossroads of Church and Chinnor Roads. At a track crossroads go R, currently signed as a footpath to Henton. After 100 - 200m on the track go L to follow the resurfaced trackbed of an old railway; an excellent, wide, flat track.

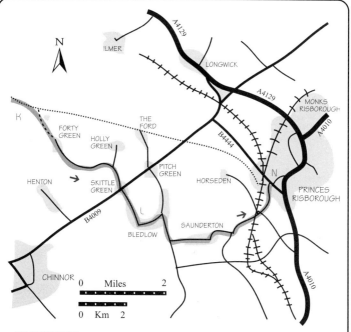

DIRECTION TIPS

K - L Follow the rail path (Sustrans improved). At the time of writing the track was blocked after 3km or so (although there are plans to extend it). Exit R at the blockage, past farm buildings on the L. This bridleway track turns to road as it passes through the thatched hamlet of Forty Green. Head straight across the B4009 and into the characterful Bledlow. Bend L in front of The Lions of Bledlow pub and pass the church.

L - N Go R at the next T-junction, signed Bledlow Ridge / Wycombe, and climb out of Bledlow. Take the next L down Oddley Lane and into Saunderton. L at the next T-junction to cross over the railway bridge. Turn L onto Picts Lane and descend into Princes Risborough to meet the B4444. Go R onto Poppy Road to meet the A4010. R here and in 100 - 200m go L onto a track (Upper Icknield Way). At the next T-junction with a road L takes you into the town centre and straight over follows the Icknield Way riders' route to the next section.

6 PRINCES RISBOROUGH - BERKHAMSTED

Section Distance Easy Option 22 miles / 35.5 km **Off-road** 10 miles /16km
Off-road Option 18 miles /29 km **Off-road** 13 miles /21 km

The Route In Princes Risborough you have the choice of a very difficult but exhilarating and largely off-road route over the Chilterns or a flatter route, on road, to Wendover, to pick up the Wendover arm of the Grand Union Canal. The latter path is also a good escape route if you have followed the mountain bike option as far as Wendover and found it too hard or muddy. **WARNING** The harder mountain bike option should only be tackled by the experienced and fit. Only attempt after a good spell of dry weather as even in good conditions there are hard climbs and tricky rutted surfaces with tree roots and stumps. In the wet it quickly becomes a quagmire (not helped by shared use with horses). You do, however, get to experience glorious Chiltern beech woods and breathtaking vistas from Whiteleaf Cross and Coombe Hill.

PRINCES RISBOROUGH TO HASTOE - HARD OFF-ROAD OPTION

• From Princes Risborough you have the option of following parts of the difficult **Icknield Way riders' route**. This takes its name from an ancient trackway, already very old when the Romans arrived. In fact it's made up of several linked paths (e.g. the upper and lower Icknield Ways) that once linked the Dorset coast and the Wash around 4,000 years ago. Named after the Iceni tribe of East Anglia who used it for trading.

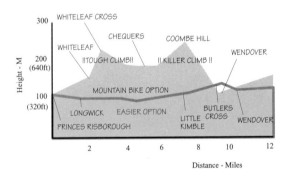

• **Whiteleaf** Tiny hamlet of gorgeous thatched cottages and convenient inn. Origin of the **giant chalk cross** above the village is uncertain; two conflicting theories are the result of someone making decorative use of a quarry around the 17th century or a much earlier military celebration of victory over the Danes. Alongside the cross lie remains of a **neolithic burial mound**, fenced off for protection. **Red Lion** Meals 12-2 & 7-9. Hook Norton, Brakespears.

• After passing behind Pulpit Hill the route goes in front of **Chequers**, traditionally the country home of British Prime Ministers. It was presented to the nation in 1917 by Lord Lee of Fareham to show his gratefulness at the ending of World War One, but isn't open to the public. Set in hundreds of acres of parkland and originally 13th century, it was rebuilt in the 15th century.

• **Coombe Hill**, highest viewpoint in the Chilterns at 852 feet. A hard climb and a short, easy walk give fantastic views of landmarks such as Chequers, Pulpit Hill and Aylesbury. Impressive Boer War monument. No bikes on footpath approach (leave them locked on bridleway track).

• **Wendover** Beautiful old village, tucked away in picturesque folds of the Chiltern Hills. Timbered cottages give historical charm and small building with clock tower and drinking fountain mark junction of Icknield Way and London-Aylesbury road. Short interesting walk to church and manor house. Latter was home of the Hampden family who refused to pay shipping tax, helping to ignite the Civil War. **Red Lion Hotel** is a fine historical inn. **Banks** Barclays, Aylesbury Rd. Lloyds, High St.

• Out of Wendover **Hale Lane** is an old drovers' road, once used to transport livestock.

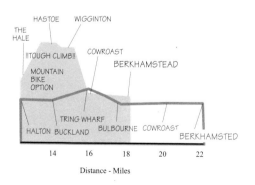

Distance - Miles

PRINCES RISBOROUGH TO HASTOE - ACCOMMODATION

Red Lion Inn, Upper Icknield Way, Whiteleaf (01844) 344476. ££££-PL-DR-LAU-SEC
Wisteria Cottage, Bowood Lane, Wendover Dean (01296) 625509 or (0411) 062288 (mobile). ££££-PL-DR-LAU-SEC. About 1 mile off the route, near Dunsmere and Little London.
17 Icknield Close, Wendover (01296) 623859. £££-DR-SEC.
46 Lionel Avenue, Wendover (01296) 623426. £££-PL-DR-LAU-SEC-WKSH.
Belton House, 26 Chiltern Rd, Wendover (01296) 622351
Dunsmore Edge, London Road, Wendover (01296) 623080
3 Lionel Avenue, Wendover (01296) 624115
36 Manor Road, Wendover (01296) 623605

HASTOE TO COWROAST - HARD OFF-ROAD OPTION

• **Tring Park** 300 beautiful acres of parkland and handsome beech trees. Once the property of the powerful Rothschild family. 18th century landscaping includes Obelisk and Summer House. Fine views to the north from the route, as it passes through the park.
• **Tring** The mansion house contains the Rothschilds' natural history collection of stuffed animals and is definitely worth a visit (includes fleas in miniature clothes!). The collection is now owned by the British Museum. Admission charge. Open 7 days a week (01442) 824181. Rothschild's Rose and Crown Inn dominates the centre of town. Shoe shop on Frogmore St. also sells bike spares.
Banks Natwest, Barclays, Midland and Link cashpoints, on the High St. Turn left on emerging at the road in Wigginton to get to Tring centre. Market day Friday.
• **Wigginton** affords great views over the Bulbourne Valley towards the northern end of the Chilterns. Greyhound pub has food. Also Cowroast Inn at Cowroast.
• **Aldbury** is just off the route, just to the east of the canal near Tring. Pretty village, handy for accommodation.
• Leave the Icknield Way to join the **Grand Union Canal**, now your companion for much of the way until you join the Thames in Greater London. Linking London and Birmingham, the canal took shape between 1793 and 1805 and was one of the key transport links that aided the Industrial Revolution. Its management was unified in the form of the Grand Union Canal Company (previously sections had been split between companies) in 1929 and heavy investment followed in an attempt to revitalise trade on the canal. It was used in World War II to carry war materials but nowadays its main role is as a leisure provider and haven for wildlife. Note the waterways code of conduct at the beginning of the book.

HASTOE TO COWROAST - ACCOMMODATION

Royal Hotel, Station Road, Tring (01442) 827616
The Crows Nest Travel Inn, Tring Hill, Tring (01442) 824819
Stocks Farmhouse, Aldbury nr. Tring (01442) 851397
16 Stoneycroft, Aldbury nr. Tring (01442) 851294
Chimanimani, Toms Hill Rd. Aldbury nr. Tring (01442) 851527
2 Church Cottages, Aldbury nr. Tring (01442) 851207

PRINCES RISBOROUGH TO WENDOVER - EASY OPTION

• Once through **Longwick** (White Horse and Red Lion pubs) you are on very quiet minor roads until **Little Kimble**, with the fine Church of All Saints containing wall paintings and 'Chertsey Tiles'. Bernard Arms pub.
• Prince of Wales pub in **Marsh**, as you turn back towards the Chilterns with great views of Coombe and Pulpit Hills ahead of you.
• The church at **Ellesborough** has a superb hillside position with extensive views over the Vale of Aylesbury. Russell Arms pub in Butlers Cross.

PRINCES RISBOROUGH TO WENDOVER - ACCOMMODATION

Red Lion, Longwick (01844) 344980
The Swan, Great Kimble (01844) 275288
For Wendover listings see previous page.

WENDOVER TO COWROAST - EASY OPTION

• **Wendover Arm, Grand Union Canal** Now filled with flora and fauna, it was once meant to act as a 'top-up' waterway for the main arm as well as being navigable. Serious leakage meant closure in 1904. The Narrows section is named so because of the concrete lining put in to stop leakage (which meant water was entering the Rothschilds' dining room nearby).
• **Halton** Unique houses grouped around the Wendover Arm, many displaying country scenes. Mainly built by the Rothschilds with beautiful bridge bearing their coat of arms.
• **Tring Reservoirs** Nineteenth century reservoirs now also managed as a 2 mile long nature reserve with large numbers of.
• **Bulbourne Junction**, where the Wendover Arm meets the main Grand Union Canal, still has an air of the canal era with its picturesque working workshops. Grand Junction Arms pub at Bulbourne.

WENDOVER TO COWROAST - ACCOMMODATION

Charterhouse, 103 London Road, Aston Clinton (01296) 631313
Baywood Guesthouse, 96 Weston Rd, Aston Clinton (01296) 630612
Hatchways, Buckland Wharf (01296) 630563

BERKHAMSTED - HISTORY AND ATTRACTIONS

• Country town, situated around the Grand Union Canal and the River Bulbourne.
Some fine buildings include the timbered Court House and Incent's House.
• The town's strong historical connections are epitomised by the **castle ruins**.
Once a residence of the Kings of Mercia, they saw Saxon nobles swearing
allegiance to William the Conqueror. Other famous owners or residents include
Henry II, Piers Gaveston, the Black Prince and a captive King John of France.
Probably finally demolished in King James's time. Just the other side of the
railway station with free admission.
• The **Church of St. Peter** dates from Norman times, with a 100ft. embattled
tower and a window dedicated to poet and hymn-writer William Cowper, born here.

BERKHAMSTED - ACCOMMODATION

Linden, Kitsbury Terrace (01442) 863275. £££-PL (in advance)-DR-LAU.
Broadway Farm (01442) 866541
The Goat Inn, High St. (01442) 866936
The Swan Inn, High St. (01442) 871451

BERKHAMSTED - OTHER INFORMATION

Market Day Saturday
Banks All major banks on High Street
⛓ **Dee's Cycles**, 317 High St. (01442) 877447

The view from above Whiteleaf Cross on the difficult mountain bike option (section 6)

Whiteleaf; a true 'chocolate box' village! (section 6)

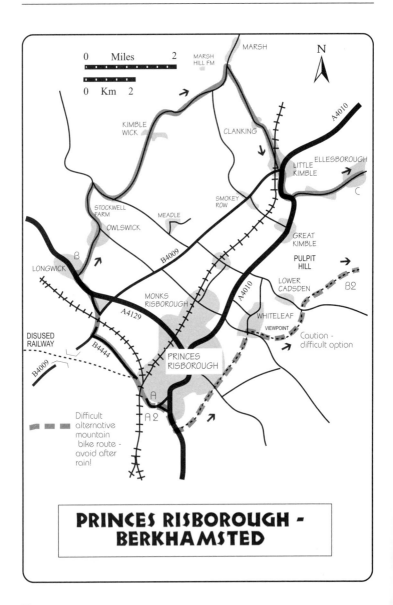

PRINCES RISBOROUGH - BERKHAMSTED

DIRECTION TIPS - PRINCES RISBOROUGH TO COWROAST - EASY OPTION

A - B CAUTION The roads followed until you turn off in Longwick are fast and can be busy. Coming into Princes Risborough on Picts Lane, meet a junction with the B4444 and go L. At the next junction with the B4009 go R (Aylesbury & Thame). Coming into Longwick under the railway bridge bear L onto the B4444 (Thame & Oxford) then L onto the busy and fast A 4129.

B - C Take the first R in Longwick, off the main road and onto Bar Lane (Owlswick & Ford). Now on a pleasant minor road, go L at the next T-junction (Owlswick & Ford) and pass through Owlswick. R at the T-junction out of Owlswick and next L at Stockwell Lane Farm (Kimble Wick, Marsh & Bishopstone). By the Prince of Wales pub bear R. This road through Clanking and into Little Kimble gives good views of Coombe Hill and the Chiltern escarpment ahead of you. L under the railway bridge then R onto the A4010, Take the next L off the A4010 onto Ellesborough Rd (Wendover).

DIRECTION TIPS - PRINCES RISBOROUGH TO COWROAST - DIFFICULT OFF-ROAD OPTION

A2 - B2 Coming into Princes Risborough on Picts Lane, meet the B4444 and go R. Bear R again onto Poppy Rd, following Icknield Way riders' route signs. At the A4010 go R. In 100-200m go L onto a track (Upper Icknield Way). At the next T-junction with a road cross straight over onto the track, continuing to follow riders route' signs (L on the road takes you into the town centre). Follow this track until meeting the next road junction and R, onto the road, to climb steeply uphill (the pretty hamlet of Whiteleaf is straight ahead at the junction). After the climb begins to level out go L into the car park for Whiteleaf Cross and pick up signs for the Ridgeway bridleway on a good track. In about 200m turn R onto a narrower bridleway, into woods, again picking up signs for the Icknield Way riders' route. CAUTION -watch out for slippy mud and roots here. Follow Riders route through the woods and emerge at the road, east of Cadsden. Cross the road and jink R, uphill, onto a difficult woodland track, again following riders' route signs.

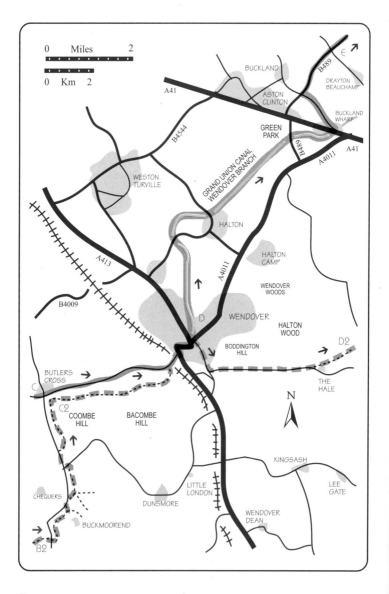

0 Miles 2

0 Km 2

BUCKLAND

B489

E

DRAYTON
BEAUCHAMP

A41

ASTON
CLINTON

BUCKLAND
WHARF

B4544

GREEN
PARK

B489

A41

A4011

GRAND UNION CANAL
WENDOVER BRANCH

WESTON
TURVILLE

HALTON

HALTON
CAMP

A413

A4011

WENDOVER
WOODS

B4009

D

WENDOVER

HALTON
WOOD

D2

BODDINGTON
HILL

BUTLERS
CROSS

THE
HALE

C

N

C2

COOMBE
HILL

BACOMBE
HILL

KINGSASH

LEE
GATE

CHEQUERS

LITTLE
LONDON

DUNSMORE

WENDOVER
DEAN

BUCKMOOREND

B2

DIRECTION TIPS - PRINCES RISBOROUGH TO COWROAST - EASY OPTION

C - D CAUTION - FAST ROAD Continue on Ellesborough Rd through Ellesborough and Butlers Cross. Continue into Wendover and over the mini-roundabout and onto the main street. At the roundabout after the clock tower go first L on the A413 for Aylesbury. R at the next mini-roundabout, onto Wharf Rd. Pick up the canal towpath on your L.

D - E Follow the canal towpath for about 5km, passing the beautiful Halton village and bridge. Leave the canal where it meets the A41 at Buckland Wharf, crossing the main road onto Buckland Rd. R at the next crossroads onto the B489 (BUSY!).

DIRECTION TIPS - PRINCES RISBOROUGH TO COWROAST - DIFFICULT OFF-ROAD OPTION

B2 - C2 This narrow and difficult woodland path passes to the right of Pulpit Hill before the track widens and you glimpse Chequers through trees, to the left (long driveways with gateway entrances lead to the house itself which is strictly private). Shortly after this view meet the road. Cross the road and immediately go L onto a narrow track, running right next to the road (still following Icknield Way riders' route signs). Just opposite a gateway entrance to Chequers, the track bends R down the side of a field and heads towards a large white property (Buckmoorend). Follow the main track just to the L of Buckmoorend, signed as the Ridgeway bridleway. Stay on the main track and start to climb uphill (ignore signs for the Icknield Way riders' route which splits off right into a field just behind the buildings). After a stiff climb of 200 - 300m come to a crossroads in the woods and go L, signed as a bridleway (R is the South Bucks Way and straight on the Ridgeway footpath). Emerge at a road and L to a T-junction where you go R (Butlers Cross and Aylesbury). In 10m head R onto a bridleway. Meeting a crossroads go straight on (bridleway down to the L and footpath up to the R). Pass a clearing with the Boer War mounument up to the R. This straight section of track appears to end at a road, by a golf course. Just through the bridleway gate here jink back acutely to the R to climb a narrow steep track. After a hard push you can leave your bikes locked up on the bridleway and follow the footpath over to the superb views from the Boer War monument on the top of Coombe Hill. Carrying on on the main track, you come to a track confluence in the woods and turn L, downhill, opposite another footpath to Coombe Hill.

C2 - D2 Descend carefully on this STEEP track to the road and R, to enter Wendover over the bypass and railway. Straight over the mini-roundabout and down the main street to bend left in front of the clock tower. At the next roundabout go R then first R signed for Hale. Follow the long straight road and as the road bends R entering the tiny settlement of The Hale go L up the track, signed Icknield Way riders' route, and onto a steep-sided track.

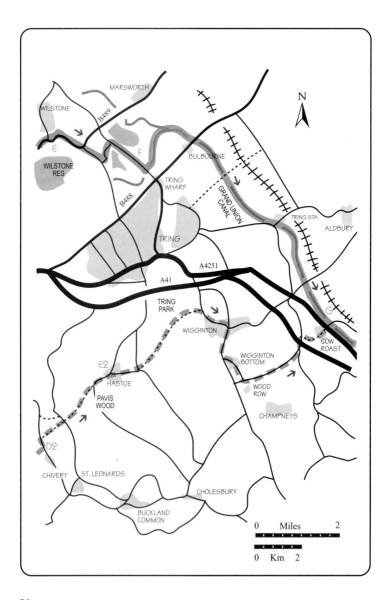

DIRECTION TIPS - PRINCES RISBOROUGH TO COWROAST - EASY OPTION

E - F Continue on the B489 for approximately 3km, over a crossroads and past a L turn for Wilstone. Take the next R turn, on a sharp L-hand bend and shortly take the next L, now on quiet minor roads. R at the next T-junction which brings you to a bridge over the Wendover branch of the Grand Union Canal, just before Tring Wharf.

F - G Go L onto the canal towpath at this bridge and continue to meet the main line of the Grand Union at Bulbourne Junction. Go R onto the towpath. Head away from Bulbourne, past the workshops and Grand Junction Arms, to meet the off-road route at Cowroast Lock and bridge, about 5km after Bulbourne Junction. Simply follow the towpath, changing over sides at bridges where necessary.

N.B. There is an excellent cycle path link from the canal to Tring centre. Come off at bridge 135, cross the canal and bear right. Pick up cycle path into Tring.

DIRECTION TIPS - PRINCES RISBOROUGH TO COWROAST - DIFFICULT OFF-ROAD OPTION

D2 - E2 Continue steeply up this difficult sunken lane, very difficult going. The Ridgeway path crosses but you stay straight on the main track to emerge at a road and L (Chivery is to the R). Continue past Chivery Reservoir and just after the road bends right go R onto the bridleway (riders' route) by Southpark House. Follow a delightful track over a field section and into woods. Now in Pavis Wood, meet the road and straight over. Pick up signs for the Ridgeway bridleway, onto a good track. Follow riders' route signs through Pavis Wood and emerge by going L onto Gadmore Lane.

E2 - G In Hastoe follow riders' route signs onto Church Lane. At the next junction go L onto Marlin Hill, signed for Tring. In 60-70m go R off the road, onto a woodland track (Woodland Trust area - Tring Park). Follow the track and at the only main junction go R. Emerge at a road and R into Wigginton on Fox Rd. In the centre of Wigginton go R onto Chesam Rd. (BEWARE - FAST ROAD). First L out of Wigginton into Wigginton Bottom. Out of Wigginton Bottom come to a T-junction and L. Descend to pass under main road. Go R just before Tinkers Lodge, onto an ungated track. Follow this bridleway in a straight line to emerge at a main road. Jink R then L to the canal at Cowroast marina. Go R over the bridge, onto the canal towpath.

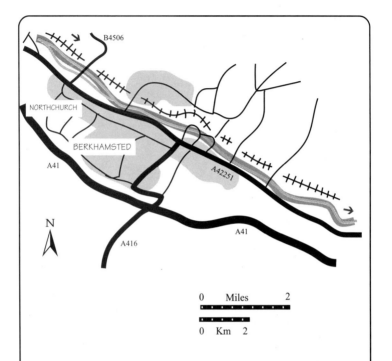

DIRECTION TIPS

After joining the canal at either Cowroast (difficult off-road option) or at Bulbourne Junction (easier road / canal option) simply follow the canal towpath in an easterly direction to come into Berkhamsted. The towpath may move from one side of the canal to the other; it is simply a case of crossing a bridge. Your entry into Berkhamsted is announced by sight of the train station on the left (near the castle).

Bridge 164 on the Grand Union, near Watford (known as Ornamental Bridge)

7 BERKHAMSTED - UXBRIDGE

Section Distance 22 miles / 35 km   **Off-road** Virtually 100%
(canal towpath and Colne Valley Trail)

The Route A well surfaced path near Berkhamsted is packed with pubs. Give way to pedestrians here due to lack of width (the path gradually widens out of Berkhamsted). After classic English scenery of church spire and cricket ground your surroundings become slightly more workaday (especially after Hemel Hempstead), although they remain overwhelmingly rural until Watford and the cycling remains flat and easy.

BERKHAMSTED TO WATFORD

• The **Rivers Bulbourne and Gade** intermingle with the Grand Union Canal in this gentle, green valley bottom. Chalky water in many of the small streams is ideal for watercress growth.
• **Winkwell Docks,** by the Three Horseshoes Pub, has been a port of call for canal boats for many years. Barge horses would be shod in the forge here.
• **Hemel Hempstead** Once a quiet and ancient market town, designated a New Town in 1947. Despite the addition of new suburbs to soak up London's excess population, the old centre retains its character. Situated on a hill above the River Gade it contains some fine buildings including the Cornmarket, parish church, town hall and bow-fronted shops. **Tourist Information**, Dacorum Information Centre, Marlowes (01442) 234222. 🚲 Hemel Hempstead Cycle Centre, 57 High St (01442) 242410. Leisure Wheels, 89 High St (01442) 213401.
• **King's Langley** Eagle Inn, Meals 12-2 & 6-8.30. Snacks and full meals up to £10.00. Cask Adnams, Bass and Shipstones plus keg Greenalls and other guest beers.

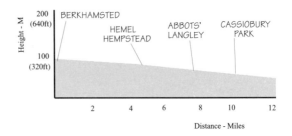

• **Grove Bridge (no. 164)**, just after passing under the M25 near Watford, is one of the most beautiful on the canal. Its white, ornamental shape was built by the canal company for the Earl of Clarendon in return for allowing the canal to pass through his estates.

ACCOMMODATION - BERKHAMSTED TO CASSIOBURY PARK

33 Rannoch Walk, Hemel Hempstead (01442) 247905
The Hawthorns, 48 Leverstock Green Rd, Hemel Hempstead (01442) 213250
47 Alexandra Rd, Hemel Hempstead (01442) 246611
Eagle Inn, Hempstead Road, King's Langley (01923) 262563. £££/£-DR-SEC
67 Hempstead Rd, King's Langley (01923) 400453

CASSIOBURY PARK TO UXBRIDGE

• The route passes through a beautiful, willow-lined section near Watford's **Cassiobury Park**, once home of the Earls of Essex.
• **Batchworth Lock** is a pretty spot centred around a pub and stables which service canal trade. The River Chess joins the canal here. Visitor centre (01923) 778382.
• **Rickmansworth** Convenient High St. shopping close to the route with small historical centre around St. Mary's Church on Church St. including The Bury mansion house (grounds open to public). The magnificent **Moor Park Mansion** lies south of Batchworth Lock. 18th century Palladian grandeur financed by South Sea Bubble profits (a national financial scandal with ministers implicated in bribery). Now a golf clubhouse but open to the public. (01923) 776611 for details. ☙ Mountain High, High St. (01923) 775630.
• **Colne Valley Park and Trail** marks the western edge of the London metropolis and the beginning of real countryside and stretches from Rickmansworth in the north to the south-west of Heathrow (the route leaves the park at Uxbridge). The route follows the waymarked Colne Valley Trail through the park from north to south, partly on canal towpath and partly on other tracks.

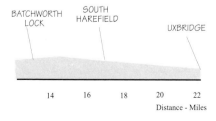

BATCHWORTH LOCK   SOUTH HAREFIELD   UXBRIDGE

14   16   18   20   22

Distance - Miles

• **Denham Country Park** is one of a number of smaller parks within Colne Valley Park and has the Colne Valley Park information office at its centre with lots of handy leaflets on the area (01895) 832662. Beautiful woodland and meadowland surround the banks of the Colne and Misbourne rivers.

• The beautifully kept village of **Denham**, like the Colne Valley Park information office, lies on a bridleway link just off the main route near **Denham Quarry**. The oldest buildings are clustered around the church and the village also boasts a number of mansions, former homes of the great and the good. The Savoy was once home of the infamous blackshirt Oswald Mosley and the grounds housed his wife's grave until 1970 when it was moved due to vandalism. Near Denham Quarry you pass through a series of former gravel pits, now enveloped by woodland and home to a variety of birds and yachts.

• **Uxbridge** marks the edge of Greater London, on the edge of the London Borough of Hillingdon (formerly in Middlesex). Convenient services along a modern high street. Unfortunately much of the old town has disappeared but the 1930s underground station is an unusual piece of tube architecture. Banks Barclays, Midland, Lloyds and Link machine on High St.

CASSIOBURY PARK TO UXBRIDGE - ACCOMMODATION

Aburi, 7 Brokengate Lane, Denham (01895) 833118. ££££-PL-DR-LAU-SEC.
8 Durrants Drive, Croxley Green, Rickmansworth (01923) 232572
30 Hazelwood Road, Croxley Green, Rickmansworth (01923) 233751
22 Moor Lane, Rickmansworth (01923) 776109
6 Swallow Close, Rickmansworth (01923) 720069
64 Valley Road, Rickmansworth (01923) 774185
Hildon Guest House, Uxbridge (01895) 231714
Ceveland Hotel, Uxbridge (01895) 257618
Spackman Guest House, Uxbridge (01895) 237994

Self-sufficiency on the Grand Union (section 7)

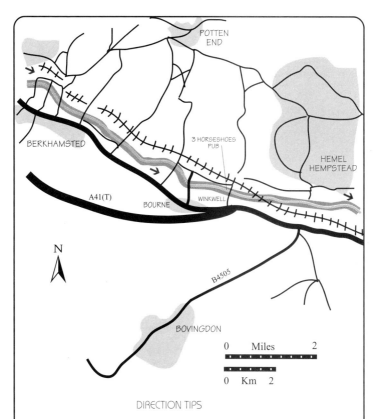

DIRECTION TIPS

It is a very easy matter to follow the canal towpath, changing banks from time to time. The main difficulty is knowing which bridge to exit at. Most bridges are numbered and a guide is given below:

No. 147. Leads to Winkwell and Bourne End on the southern side. (Swing bridge by the Three Horseshoes)
Nos. 150 & 151. The two bridges after the Fishery Inn bridge. Both roads lead north into Hemel Hempstead.

BERKHAMSTED - UXBRIDGE

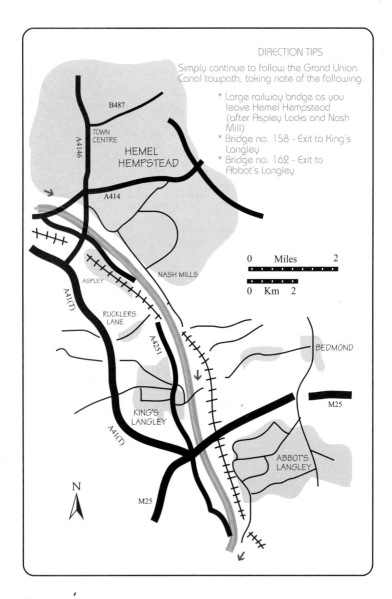

DIRECTION TIPS

Simply continue to follow the Grand Union Canal towpath, taking note of the following:

* Large railway bridge as you leave Hemel Hempstead (after Aspley Locks and Nash Mill)
* Bridge no. 158 - Exit to King's Langley
* Bridge no. 162 - Exit to Abbot's Langley

B487

TOWN CENTRE

A4146

HEMEL HEMPSTEAD

A414

NASH MILLS

0   Miles   2

0   Km   2

ASPLEY

A41(T)

RUCKLERS LANE

A4251

BEDMOND

M25

KING'S LANGLEY

A41(T)

ABBOT'S LANGLEY

N

M25

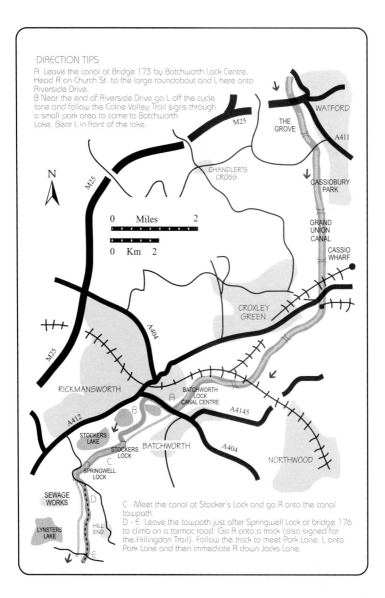

DIRECTION TIPS

A Leave the canal at Bridge 173 by Batchworth Lock Centre.
Head R on Church St. to the large roundabout and L here onto
Riverside Drive.
B Near the end of Riverside Drive go L off the cycle
lane and follow the Colne Valley Trail signs through
a small park area to come to Batchworth
Lake. Bear L in front of the lake.

N

0   Miles   2

0   Km   2

WATFORD

THE
GROVE

A411

CHANDLER'S
CROSS

M25

CASSIOBURY
PARK

GRAND
UNION
CANAL

CASSIO
WHARF

CROXLEY
GREEN

M25

A404

RICKMANSWORTH

A412

BATCHWORTH
LOCK
CANAL CENTRE

A4145

STOCKERS
LAKE

STOCKERS
LOCK

BATCHWORTH

A404

NORTHWOOD

SPRINGWELL
LOCK

SEWAGE
WORKS

HILL
END

LYNSTERS
LAKE

C   Meet the canal at Stocker's Lock and go R onto the canal
towpath.
D - E Leave the towpath just after Springwell Lock at bridge 176
to climb on a tarmac road. Go R onto a track (also signed for
the Hillingdon Trail). Follow the track to meet Park Lane. L onto
Park Lane and then immediate R down Jacks Lane.

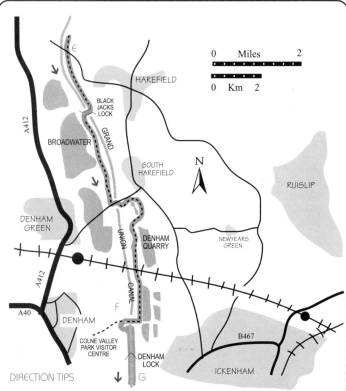

DIRECTION TIPS

E - F Continue down Jacks Lane. It becomes an unsurfaced track to meet Black Jacks Lock on the Grand Union Canal. Cross over the canal and head L down the wide track (not the towpath). Emerge onto the road by the Horse & Barge pub. Go L over the canal and in 150m go R into the car park. Join the Quarry Trail at the rear of the car park and over a tarmac road to rejoin the trail. Bend L to pass between the canal on the R and lakes on the L.

F - G Head over the short pedestrian bridge (white, no.182) on your R and L back onto the canal towpath. Just over the bridge you may want to detour into Denham or to Colne Valley Park visitor centre (canalside map).

Berkhamsted Castle (section 7)

Taking a break at Batchworth Lock (section 7)

8 UXBRIDGE - PUTNEY

Section Distance 22.5 miles / 36km   **Off-road** Almost entirely off-road
(very few sections on minor road)

The Route Continuing on the Grand Union Canal from Uxbridge provides a
fine countryside route until the urban environment begins to intrude around
Yiewsley. The towpath is generally good quality except for the section between
Bull's Bridge and Norwood Top Lock (adjacent roads should be used as shown
on the map) although it may become muddy and puddled after heavy rain. The
route retains its pleasant, natural character along much of its length, through
Brent River Park, Syon House grounds and by the Thames. Planes using
Heathrow airport pass at what seems a lazy pace, low enough for you to read
their logos. It would be quite easy to forget you are near the centre of a major
world capital without such reminders of civilisation. You follow a different route
to the outward leg through Richmond Park before retracing your outward steps
back to Putney Bridge.

UXBRIDGE TO BRENTFORD

• The **Grand Union Canal** immediately after Uxbridge remains a green corridor
dotted with pubs; the **Dolphin** and **General Elliot** (Uxbridge), the **Shovel** and
Turning Point (Cowley), **De Burgh Arms** (West Drayton), the **Blue Anchor**
and **Old Crown** (Hayes), the **Grand Junction Arms** and **Old Oak Tree**
(Southall). Through Yiewsley, Hayes, Drayton and Southall housing and industry
have the edge before nature once again reigns in **Brent River Park**. Despite
the occasional intrusion of canalside factories wildlife still abounds with water
lilies and herons amongst many other species. At **Bull's Bridge** the canal
splits; left for the Paddington Arm (linking to Regent's Canal and the Thames)

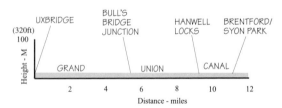

and straight on to Brentford (our route). This area was once a repair yard and the canal would have been busy with glass, bricks and timber going into the centre and rubbish coming out. The decline of the canal as a means of transport has meant an upsurge in 'regeneration' leisure and development plans; works may have started near Bull's Bridge or near Brentford High Street by the time you ride this section. 🚲 Bicycle Warehouse, 209 Kingshill Av., Hayes (0181) 8412595. Hayes Cycle Centre, 13 Coldharbour Lane (0181) 5732402.

• Interesting canal architecture includes the flight of **six locks at Hanwell** (a Scheduled Ancient Monument) and **Three Bridges** just before the locks (an intersection of road, rail and canal).

• **Brentford Musical Museum**, 368 High St. (0181) 5608108

• **Syon House** Built on the site of a monastery, the Tudor house contains amazing Robert Adam plaster interiors surrounded by a Capability Brown landscaped garden. The huge greenhouse with amazing glass and metalwork is a must. The house has been in the possession of the Earls of Northumberland since the 17th century. Surrounding attractions include butterfly house, trout fishery and aquatic experience animal display. Gift shop, cafe and wholefood store. Open April - October. For times and admission charges ring (0181) 5600881.

UXBRIDGE TO BRENTFORD - ACCOMMODATION

Balmoral Guest House, 263 Balmoral Drive, Hayes (0181) 7971692. ££££. Breakfast £2.50.
Lyttleton Lodge, Cowley, Uxbridge (01895) 254970
Ashley Lodge Guest House, Hayes (0181) 5691586
Oakdene Guest House, Hayes (0181) 5730750
152 Cranborne Waye, Hayes (0181) 5690166
Maygoods Farm, Cowley, Uxbridge (01895) 233105

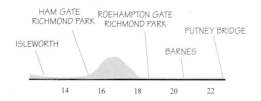

BRENTFORD TO PUTNEY

• **Old Isleworth**, neat and pretty, precedes your meeting of the **Thames Path** (a section of the long-distance footpath that is open to cyclists). At **Richmond Bridge** you must decide if you want to take the ferry option or whether you want to cross the bridge and use the other bank of the Thames. The beautiful five-arched bridge is preceded by the picturesque **Richmond Lock**.

• **Richmond** itself is a spectacle worth the short diversion off the route. Carry on over Richmond Bridge and go left up Hill Street to the centre. The **Green**, just to the north-west is a beautiful open area surrounded by grand houses. The gateway to Henry VII's palace is still by The Green. Nice walk through Old Palace Yard to river. **Tourist Information**, Whittaker Av, (0181) 9409125, is adjacent to Richmond Museum. Admission charge. (0181) 3321141. **Banks** Main branches around George St. and The Quadrant. ⬭ Super Cycles, 219 Lower Mortlake Rd. (0181) 9403717.

• If on the ferry option you will see **Marble Hill House** on your right, just before the boat. This eighteenth century house is open to the public (0181) 8925115. If you carry on past the ferry you will see the elegant **Orleans House Gallery** up to the right, housing the borough art collection and temporary exhibitions.

• The route passes in front of the gates of **Ham House**, yet another splendid residence open to the public. Once acclaimed as one of the most lavish houses in the country, crammed full of continental craftsmanship. Admission charge (National Trust) (0181) 9401950. In the days when Richmond was the monarch's personal playground many nobles had luxurious residences built in the area in an attempt to follow the royal court at leisure.

• Going through **Richmond Park**, on a different route second time around reveals a new set of attractions. You follow the Tasmin Trail around the edge of the park. **Pembroke Lodge** boasts a cafe and restaurant. Superb views from the terraced garden across London to the Chilterns. The Mound has an unusual keyhole view, through holly hedging, of St. Paul's Cathedral and The City.

⬭ Original Bicycle Hire Co. nr. Roehampton Gate, Richmond Park (0777) 5884848.

• Out of Richmond Park at Roehampton Gate you retrace the outward route back to Putney Bridge; see details on this area on pages 16-17.

BRENTFORD TO PUTNEY - ACCOMMODATION

Anna Guest House, 36-38 Church Road, Richmond (0181) 9405237
Shandon House, 37 Church Road, Richmond (0181) 9405000
4 Church Road, Richmond (0181) 9485852
446 Upper Richmond Road West, Richmond (0181) 8783268
Idono, 41 Church Road, Richmond (0181) 9485852
21 Vicarage Road, East Sheen (0181) 8766516
3 Ferry Road, Barnes (0181) 7481561

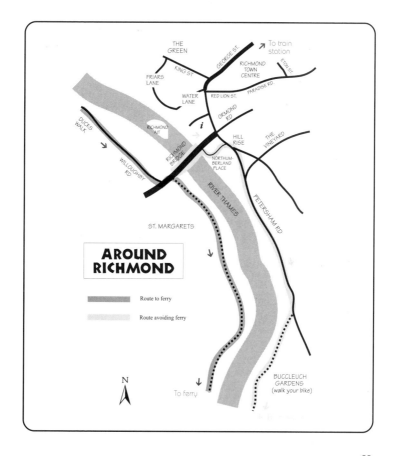

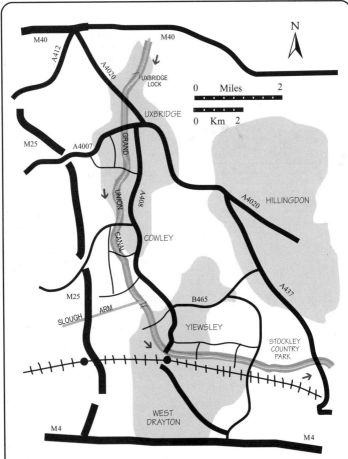

DIRECTION TIPS

Just follow the Grand Union Canal towpath! To get to Uxbridge centre exit the towpath on the bridge after Uxbridge Lock and head L into the town centre.

UXBRIDGE - PUTNEY BRIDGE

DIRECTION TIPS

Simply follow the canal towpath. Follow British Waterways advice
on the following sections:

BULL'S BRIDGE TO NORWOOD TOP LOCK - Where towpath is narrow and
restricted use roads immediately adjacent to the canal if possible.
ALONGSIDE HANWELL LOCK FLIGHT - Dismount.

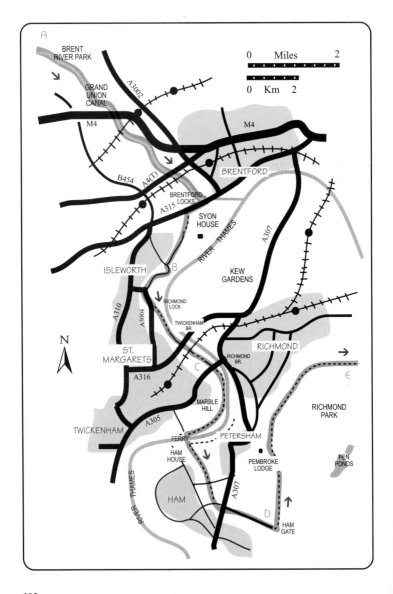

DIRECTION TIPS

A - B
Follow the canal path through Brent River Park to Brentford High St, passing the following on the way: Osterley Lock / M4 motorway bridge / railway bridge / weir / berth covered in corrugated iron / Brentford Locks and marina. Head R onto the main road through Brentford. Just past Brent Lea on the L take the next L down the pedestrian entrance (actually a road used as a public path - cycling is allowed). Continue on the road through the car park, past Syon House on the L. At the exit go L to come alongside the Thames.

B - C
Stay on Church Street through Old Isleworth, bearing L to come to a T-junction with Swan St. and R. Meet the main Richmond Road and go L. Continue through a mini-roundabout to pass Nazareth House on the L. Turn off the main road down Railshead Rd, past Brunel University to come alongside the Thames on a path. Continue onto the quiet road by Richmond Lock then first L under Twickenham Bridge. Follow Ducks Walk as it becomes Willoughby Road and ends on the southern side of Richmond Bridge.

C - D
FERRY OPTION (shorter option)
Go straight across the southern end of Richmond Bridge and onto the riverside path. Follow the path past Marble Hill park and take the small ferry across the River Thames.
NON-FERRY OPTION
Go L across Richmond Bridge. Over the bridge head R up Hill Rise then R onto Petersham Road. Descend on the road and go R, just after the Three Pigeons Pub wheeling your bike through Buccleuch Gardens and remounting on the riverside path. (Note -from here to the ferry is not yet an official cycle path. It may be very busy with pedestrians, so please ride carefully).
From the ferry terminus on the southern bank of the Thames (where both options meet) head off the main track through a small patch of woods and onto the track in front of Ham House. Head L alongside the brick wall on your R (track runs alongside horse track). At the end of the wall head R across grass and scrub land onto another track, with the rear gates of Ham House directly behind you. Go across a minor road and continue on the track until meeting the road in front of Ham Green and its pond. Go L on The Common to a crossroads and straight across onto Ham Gate Avenue (path). Carry on through Ham Gate into Richmond Park. (Note: gates may occasionally be closed at times of the deer cull - contact 0181 9483209 for full details.)

D - E
Pick up the sandy cycle track at the side of the road. Go L on the track at the next crossroads (signed Richmond Gate). Ascend to Pembroke Lodge then continue on the obvious cycle track to pass Richmond Gate on the L.

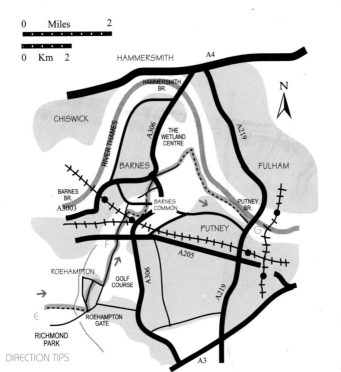

DIRECTION TIPS

E - F Continue on the cycle track through Richmond Park, passing Bishop,
Cambrian, Bog and Sheen gates. Exit the park at Roehampton Gate. Go
immediate L up Roehampton Gate (street), now retracing the outward route.
Go R then L at successive T-junctions to come onto the pavement cycle track
on Priory Lane. Follow the track to the main crossroads with Upper Richmond Rd.

F - G Go straight across onto Vine Road cycle track. Immediately over the
second level crossing go R onto a track alongside a cricket ground and emerge
at the road by Barnes station. Go R onto the road and, emerging at the junction
with the major Rocks Lane, head L on the path across Barnes Common. Head
straight across Mill Lane and across another patch of common. Emerge at a road
and jink R then L up Elm Grove Rd. At the major junction head across the main
road onto Queen Elizabeth Walk. Pass the Wetland Centre and continue to the
Thames. R onto the riverside path and continue as the path becomes road to
meet Putney Bridge.

INDEX

CITIES, TOWNS, VILLAGES & PLACES IN MAIN TEXT

Entries in red type indicate town maps

ACCOMMODATION / CAMPING INDEX

Λ at the end of an accommodation section indicates camping site.

ABOUT THE AUTHOR

Richard Peace is a freelance author and photographer. He was educated at
Queen Elizabeth Grammar School, Wakefield and Magdalen College, Oxford.
After several periods of foreign travel he qualified as a solicitor and began
outdoor writing as a hobby during his time in a solicitor's office. He has eleven
titles to his name. He has also written for several national outdoor magazines.

OTHER BOOKS BY RICHARD PEACE

All guides are illustrated with either drawings or black and white photos and come complete
with sketch maps and lots of other practical information.

CYCLING GUIDES

THE ULTIMATE C2C GUIDE £6.95 ISBN 1-901464-02-4
Excellent Books
Simply the most popular long distance cycling route in the UK, completed by
thousands each year. From the Cumbrian coast to Newcastle or Sunderland.

YORKSHIRE DALES CYCLE WAY £5.50 ISBN 1-870141-28-8
Hillside Publications
An outstanding 130 mile route circling the entire national park. Beginning in the
market town of Skipton. Malham, Settle, Dent, and Swaledale precede a superb
return to Grassington. Minor roads follow leafy dales and cross open moorland.

WEST YORKSHIRE CYCLE WAY £4.99 ISBN 1-870141-38-5
Hillside Publications
This 152 mile route starts in Haworth and takes in many of the contrasts of
West Yorkshire, from pastoral plains to rolling Pennine scenery. Visit Otley
Chevin, Pontefract Castle, Aberford and the Worth and Holme Valleys.

MOUNTAIN BIKING WEST AND SOUTH YORKSHIRE £5.99
ISBN 1-870141-40-7 Hillside Publications
20 rides, 8.5 to 16.5 miles, from the high Pennines to the rolling eastern plains.
Includes Ilkley Moor, Calderdale, Holme Valley and Barnsley Canal.

THE ULTIMATE WEST COUNTRY WAY GUIDE £8.95
ISBN 1-901464-03-2 Excellent Books
152 pages packed with information and pictures on this 250 mile Sustrans
route through the best of the south-west.

BIKING COUNTRY GLASGOW, CLYDE VALLEY AND LOCH LOMOND £5.99
ISBN 1-870141-45-8 Hillside Publications
18 well-researched and attractive routes exploring the hidden corners around
Glasgow. Using canal towpaths, special cycle tracks, farm tracks and minor
roads, the routes range from 6 to 18 miles.

MOUNTAIN BIKE LANCASHIRE AND SOUTH PENNINES £5.99
ISBN 1-901464-00-8 Excellent Books
20 off-road routes, visiting numerous scenic highlights in the Red Rose County
and South Pennines. 6.5 to 20 miles to suit all levels of mountain biker. Includes
famed scenery such as the Bowland Fells and Pendle Witch Country.

LEISURE RIDES IN THE PEAK DISTRICT AND DERBYSHIRE £5.95
ISBN 1-901464-01-6 Excellent Books
25 trails and circular routes in the Peak District and Derbyshire. Ideal for families
and occasional / leisure riders. Many moderate length outings with longer
linear outings allowing you to do as much or as little as you like. Practical
advice on cycling with children plus cycle hire and eating details. Routes cover
the Dark and the White Peak areas and visitor attractions such as Chatsworth.

WALKING AND GENERAL GUIDES

YORK WALKS £2.50 ISBN 1-870141-47-4 Hillside Publications
5 classic walks around the city of York exploring the major tourist sites and
many lesser known features. Each theme walk traces an aspect of the York
story over the centuries. Includes children's attractions and historic inns.

THE MACLEHOSE TRAIL AND ITS SURROUNDINGS £7.99
ISBN 962-7335-14-2 The Alternative Press, Hong Kong
Written during the author's period in Hong Kong teaching English, this is a
complete practical guide to the superb 100 kilometre walking trail that crosses
the mountainous New Territories of Hong Kong. A superb blend of cityscape
and wild countryside add up to a once in-a-lifetime experience.

LANCASHIRE CURIOSITIES £6.95
ISBN 1-874336-42-3 The Dovecote Press
This popular series from the Dovecote Press looks at follies, buildings and all
things curious on a county by county basis. 80 interesting sites county-wide,
profusely illustrated with quality black and white photographs.

*THE ABOVE BOOKS MAY BE OBTAINED AT ALL GOOD BOOK SHOPS OR DIRECT
FROM EXCELLENT BOOKS (DETAILS AT FRONT OF BOOK).*